THE EIGHTH EARL OF ELGIN

JAMES BRUCE, EARL OF ELGIN AND KINCARDINE, K.T
From the Portrait by George Richmond, R.A

THE
EIGHTH EARL OF ELGIN

A CHAPTER
IN NINETEENTH-CENTURY
IMPERIAL HISTORY

By
J. L. MORISON, D.Litt.

PROFESSOR OF MODERN HISTORY IN ARMSTRONG COLLEGE,
THE UNIVERSITY OF DURHAM.
AUTHOR OF "BRITISH SUPREMACY AND
CANADIAN SELF-GOVERNMENT."

GREENWOOD PRESS, PUBLISHERS
WESTPORT, CONNECTICUT

Originally published in 1928
by Hodder and Stoughton, Ltd., London

Reprinted from an original copy in the collections
of the Brooklyn Public Library

First Greenwood Reprinting 1970

Library of Congress Catalogue Card Number 73-109798

SBN 8371-4289-X

Printed in the United States of America

TO
MY WIFE

PREFACE

WHEN the Canadian History Society was founded in 1923, it included among its objects the publication of biographies " of those who have by their services contributed to the history of the country."

The present volume is the first of these biographies, and no one who is familiar with Canadian history will deny that the eighth Earl of Elgin is entitled to a foremost place. It would be difficult, even if we were to include Champlain and Frontenac as possible rivals, to name another Governor of European training whose work has proved so decisive and permanent as that of the man who, more even than the Earl of Durham, indicated the lines along which modern Canada should develop.

In writing the book I have ventured to stray from the beaten track in two ways. In the first place, the biography is not confined to the Canadian Governor-Generalship of Lord Elgin. In early Victorian days the separate parts of the Empire were bound together, not only by a common policy and moral purpose, but by the service rendered in one after another of the scattered parts by certain great servants of the Queen— George Grey for example in Australia and South Africa as well as in New Zealand, and Charles Metcalfe in India, Jamaica and Canada. It would have taken from this study of Lord Elgin's career something of its full meaning, even for Canada, had I neglected his apprenticeship in Jamaica, or the work in China, Japan, and India, in which he used the experience acquired in North America.

In the second place, it has seemed best not to write another personal life of the individual, James Bruce, but to deal with him frankly as a great public servant of the Queen, facing, in both West and East, some of the acutest difficulties ever presented by Imperial administration, and giving literally all his maturer years, and his life itself, to their solution. One may do this with the lighter conscience, since Theodore Walrond's authoritative personal biography has left little unsaid. After testing Walrond's book throughout its whole extent by reference to original authorities, I can find no fault with its fidelity to facts, and only once have I detected a slight error in judgment in the handling of his sources. My endeavour has been to write

PREFACE

a series of political studies, based mainly on Lord Elgin's public and private papers.

I have to thank Sir Campbell Stuart, who imposed upon me the pleasant duty of writing the book, and the editors of the *Cambridge Historical Journal* for permitting me to include in Chapter VII material published in that periodical, entitled " Lord Elgin in India, 1862–63." I find it difficult to express my debt to the present Earl of Elgin, for the generous freedom with which he has placed the Elgin papers at my disposal, and the courtesy which did not weary of my importunities.

J. L. MORISON.

DILSTON CROSSING,
CORBRIDGE,
NORTHUMBERLAND,
July 5, 1927.

CONTENTS

ILLUSTRATIONS

CHAPTER I

IMPERIAL PROBLEMS IN THE VIC-
TORIAN ERA; THE BEGINNING OF
LORD ELGIN'S CAREER

THE chief determining factor in modern British imperial history was the astonishing increase in the population between 1815 and the middle of the century, reinforced by the corresponding growth of British trade. This, in colonial as well as in domestic affairs, constituted an " English Revolution " as sweeping and glorious as anything in the seventeenth century : for it involved changes, not controlled by human ingenuity or energy, but imposed on men by overwhelming physical facts, and advancing with the steady march of the laws of nature. As a direct consequence of these changes, there came into existence a new British Empire. It is customary to look back to the sixteenth and seventeenth centuries for the roots of British colonization, but for working purposes the Empire, as we know it, came into existence after 1815, and its prime cause was this revolution caused by the growth of the population, and the influence on the people of mechanical inventions.

Empires are created not so much through individual adventures, or isolated conquests, as by folk-wanderings, and the British people did not really start on their travels as a people until after Waterloo. There had indeed been the preliminary experiment on the sea-board of North America, but only a few inspired or eccentric minds, Burke's for example, or Chatham's, regarded that as anything but an external excrescence on the life of England. And it ended, as it was bound to end, in separation. In the new expansion, however, it was plainly the country as a whole which was in movement. Individuals like Gibbon Wakefield might devise schemes which served useful temporary purposes, but conscious effort and intention played a very small part in all that happened.

Restless and dissatisfied individuals of every class, hampered by the overcrowding and competition which existed in all the chief centres of population, fled from the fretting strain ; and if they found the struggle for existence grimmer and even more desperate in Australia and Canada, at least it was a fight with enemies which could be grappled with—virgin country, and hard physical work, and the old struggle to organize the crude resources of nature into a means of providing food and clothing, not a hopeless attempt to escape strangulation by intangible and complicated economic law.

Everywhere, from Cape Wrath to Cornwall, and from Norfolk to Connemara, the revolution operated with that free wastage of life and individual comfort, that prodigality of effort to which no definite and immediate results seemed to come in answer, and yet in the end that growth of positive and permanent benefits, which always accompany a change created by nature and uncontrollable by human plan. The barest record of what the colonial revolution achieved lies in estimates of the population in the chief colonies of Britain before 1870. At the time of Confederation there were over 3,350,000 inhabitants in British North America ; about the same time in Australia almost 1,200,000 ; in 1858 New Zealand had 60,000 settlers, in 1867, 218,000 ; and between 1821 and the census of 1865, the white population of Cape Colony had increased from 50,000 to 250,000.[1]

The same half century of expansion saw an emigration of four millions, mainly Irish, from the British Islands to the United States.[2]

The revolution had its commercial, as well as

[1] Figures taken from colonial year-books: in the case of South Africa from Noble : *Descriptive Handbook of the Cape Colony* (1875), based on the census of 1865

[2] Johnson, *Emigration from the U.K. to North America*, pp. 344–5.

15

its merely human side. The British population could no longer be maintained from home supplies, no matter what the defenders of Corn Laws might contend. That meant importation of food. To pay for national purchases, iron and cotton and woollen industries struggled to force their wares on reluctant foreign markets ; and, once more, because raw material, either non-existent in Britain, or too scantily produced there, was needed in the workshop, new avenues for importation were cleared, and once more the imports had to be met with exports. Apart, however, from any moderate and balanced economic exchange, there was also the restlessness of the pioneering element in trade. As men fled from Scottish and English homes in pursuit of a comfort and independence which they had never tried to define for themselves, and to which, indeed, they were never to attain, so in South America, Africa and China, they clamoured at shut doors, or pushed through forbidden entrances, inspired by the mere excitement of the venture. Trade had not yet had the romance or adventure of it extinguished by modern processes ; and in its own subdued way early Victorian trade was not a whit behind that of Elizabethan and Stuart times, in the risk it took the lives it freely spent, and the contempt of all law, human and divine, with which it was sometimes accompanied.

This irrepressible Victorian expansion overseas could not but create problems of equally great dimensions ; but these questions must not be regarded as unnatural, or, in the narrow sense of the word, regrettable ; they were the ordinary consequences of a sudden but natural growth. It was the familiar story of old bottles and new wine. About the time when Victoria ascended the throne, at least three of these problems had become troublesome ; but the acuteness of them will be understood only if they are stated, not as dried constitutional, or international, or economic formulæ, but as essentially common human events.

In the first place, there was the difficulty of supervising the new overseas population. The government of Great Britain had been planned on insular, or, at best, on European lines ; and in a world confessedly imperfect it had served its purpose wonderfully well. Its colonial policy, apart from the failure to comprehend the meaning and character of the old American colonies, had roughly met the needs of African trade settlements, and West Indian plantations. It had also provided for the control of certain conquests, made from European rivals, the full implications of the possession of which had happily not been forced too suddenly on the bureaucracy at home. The root of the trouble lay in the political temper of the ordinary Englishman, that temper being, not changed, but only reinforced, by passage overseas. The difficulty naturally arose first in the North American settlements. England had done as much for these colonies as any mother-country could have been expected to do ; had given them a most generous support with army and navy ; financed them when in difficulties ; provided them with laws ; and sent them governors, who although by no means Plato's philosopher-kings, had usually possessed ordinary British qualities of honesty and resolution. Nevertheless the home government had failed to understand that such benevolent but superimposed assistance was still not of the essence of true colonial government. A group of settlers cleared their district. Government in the first instance meant chiefly self-protection, and the organization of supplies. That they provided for themselves. Then the groups grew into communities, and the communities developed mutual communications. Still the main functions of government had to be exercised by the settlers ; for government was not a thing of books and offices, or even laws, but of meeting common needs with some immediate answer. They alone knew the nature of the needs, and they alone were competent to satisfy them. There was no question of genius, or political ideals, or

incorrupt wisdom. Plain men and women, struggling for existence, knew only one form of government, and it was heroically democratic. No doubt
their pioneer struggles had always been immensely
assisted from outside—in this case by the British
Government ; but gratitude for assistance was perfectly compatible with the most complete refusal to
yield a single point in individual rights or freedom
of action. As the overflow of population converted
the scattered settlements into provinces, not entirely
uncivilized, and the need for more complicated
forms of government increased, it still remained
true that, willing to take whatever a benevolent
mother country might give, and to ask for more,
recognizing dimly their unfitness for extended
operations in government, impinged on in their
remote settlements by external influences against
which they were powerless, and with which the
home government alone could adequately grapple,
the colonists still held that only they themselves
knew what they wanted, and only they could
satisfy their own demands. The presence of so-
called Loyalist or Tory aristocracies, as in Upper
Canada, proclaiming the duty of the settlers
towards the imperial centre, was merely an odd
perversion of the same demand for autonomy, for
the true colonial aristocrat never thought of the
British Government except in terms of his own

set. His vision of imperial control was a colonial administration with all the powers and emoluments in the hands of himself and his fellow-loyalists. The first problem presented by the revolution, then, was this. Given a superintending English government, generous towards its colonies, immensely better disciplined than anything which the colonists could improvise, usually incorrupt, and conscious that for long the youthful colonies dare not face, for themselves, the difficulties thrust on them by alien neighbours ; given, on the other hand, groups of Englishmen, Scotsmen and Irishmen whose presence overseas was itself a proof that they had energy and independence above the average, learned, not in political science or literature, but in mere living, clumsy, poor, and naturally self-regarding not to say corrupt in the management of communal affairs, by what stages could the legal political control be vested in colonial hands, and what means were calculated to retain the increasingly independent state in connection with the imperial centre ?

The second difficulty created by the revolution was one of ethics ; it was a consequence of trade expansion. By whatever arguments maintained, the moral responsibility of a Government towards its subjects has long ago been as a postulate except in the school of Machiavelli. But trade has seldom

accepted the shackles of moral law, except where
moral law has obviously made for commercial
prosperity. If Machiavelli were alive to bring *Il
Principe* up to date, he would call his book " The
Merchant." From the days when John Hawkins
found African negroes good commerce, down to
the success of the most recent American combine,
this disconnection of trade from moral standards
has prevailed. It does not mean that traders
overseas have been worse than ordinary men,
but only that human nature is rarely moral in
its behaviour under new conditions, or when
inspired by merely self-regarding motives. In
British history the problem occurred for the first
time in unusual proportions after Clive had given
the East India Company extended opportunities
for profits. Burke may in many things be counted
a prejudiced witness, but no one has ever con-
tradicted the terrible indictment which he drew
up against the trading government of the East
India Company in 1783 :

" Our conquest there, after twenty years, is as crude as
it was in the first day. The natives scarcely know what
it is to see the grey head of an Englishman. Young men
(boys almost) govern there, without society, and without
sympathy with the natives. They have no more social
habits with the people than if they still resided in England ; nor, indeed, any species of intercourse but that
which is necessary to making a sudden fortune, with a

view to a remote settlement. Animated with all the avarice of age, and all the impetuosity of youth, they roll in one after another, wave after wave ; and there is nothing before the eyes of the natives but an endless, hopeless prospect of new flights of birds of prey and passage, with appetites continually renewing for a food that is continually wasting. Every rupee of profit made by an Englishman is lost for ever to India. With us are no retributory superstitions by which a foundation of charity compensates, through ages, to the poor, for the rapine and injustice of a day. With us, no pride erects stately monuments which repair the mischiefs which pride had produced, and which adorn a country out of its own spoils. England has erected no churches, no hospitals, no palaces, no schools ; England has built no bridges, made no high roads, cut no navigations, dug out no reservoirs. Every other conqueror of every other description has left some monument, either of state or beneficence, behind him. Were we to be driven out of India this day, nothing would remain to tell that it had been possessed, during the inglorious period of our dominion, by anything better than the ourang-outang, or the tiger." [1]

The process was still continuing in the nineteenth century, although no longer to the same extent in India. The chief justification for the annexation of New Zealand was that it snatched the islands from the uncovenanted mercies of the wandering trader. In spite of Livingstone's vision of Africa civilized by Christian trade, the history of that continent cannot be held to be complimen-

[1] Speech on Mr. Fox's East India Bill.

tary to commercial morality, and the subject of
this study used language of singular gravity as,
again and again, he reported in private letters his
impressions of the ever-increasing contact between
Eastern communities and Western trade :

" Can I do anything to prevent England from calling
down on herself God's curses for brutalities committed
on another feeble Oriental race ? Or are all my exertions to result only in the extension of the area over which
Englishmen are to exhibit how hollow and superficial are
both their civilization and their Christianity? The tone
of the two or three men connected with mercantile houses
in China whom I find on board is all for blood and massacre on a great scale." [1]

It was an evil of vast complexity. No valid
reason could be found against the free expansion
of British foreign trade ; yet the vanguard of the
trade advance was always composed of those who
recked least of justice and mercy. The trader,
too, in earlier stages of his work, was not infre-
quently ill treated by his prospective customers,
and his excesses were easily explained, if not
excused, by the bad faith and heartless cruelty of
his hosts. It was difficult for the governments, both
of the country trading and of the country pur-
chasing, to control their subjects, or to enter into

[1] *Letters to Lady Elgin*, 22 May, 1860. This title is used to
describe a privately printed volume of Lord Elgin's letters to
his wife between 1847 and 1862.

some compact with each other which might assume the dignity of international law. Commerce, as soon as it leaves the domestic sphere, becomes really a branch of government ; what we call empire is as much the expansion of national trade, as it is the over-seas settlement of British subjects ; but apart altogether from the disinclination of politicians to recognize this fact, there are the enormous obstacles that, as often as not, the trade is conducted at the ends of the earth, and with races of inferior or strange forms of civilization, and that the strange government has usually preferred the absence of agreement, to the legalizing and civilizing of the trade contact.

The third problem was that of nationality, or, stated in its primary form, race. Two hundred and fifty years of incessant activity had involved Great Britain deeply in national and racial difficulties.

These existed in the most diverse of forms. In the West Indies, a people once counted barely human had first been imported like cattle to meet agrarian and mechanical needs ; then they had received their freedom ; and, as their numbers were so much greater than those of the white governing and owning classes, their prospective admission to the franchise at once raised the race question over its entire extent. In India a meagre

minority of traders, governors, and soldiers dominated a mass of brown men, counting not in tens,
but in hundreds of millions ; and men like Charles
Metcalfe, who had spent a lifetime in governing
this alien population, realized how slight the
connection between England and India was, and
what catastrophic results might flow from even
the slightest diminution of British prestige. The
trifling academic question whether the Indian
Mutiny was a national revolt, or a military rising,
may be ignored. The truth was that India had
never acquiesced in English lordship, and the
Anglo-Indian government had to grapple with
the double question of making a modern constitution which should induce unwilling Hindus
and Moslems to accept the rule which circumstances
had imposed upon them.

In South Africa and Canada, nationality
appeared in a more comprehensible and therefore
practicable form. In former days, when dynasties
held all the power, and populations were at best
intractable partners in furnishing men and money
for dynastic wars, it was natural for sections of a
population to be handed over to the victor as
the price of peace. It was fitting that gentlemen
should pay their honourable debts ; and so when
the gentlemen of England defeated those of France,
a population in Quebec counting some tens of

thousands, French in every detail, and with their religion reinforcing their nationality, suddenly became British in the eyes of international law. By another " gentleman's agreement," the King of Holland entered on his new duties in 1815, comfortably well-off, because Great Britain had purchased Dutch South Africa, after conquering it. No doubt the chief importance of the new colony lay in its position on the road to India ; but it happened to be occupied by some thousands of Dutch inhabitants, and they in turn were engulfed in a constantly increasing population of African natives. To relate the race question to British policy would lead too far afield : it will suffice to deal with the minor phase of nationality. Under British rule the conquered or purchased populations flourished greatly, and, as often as not, if there was friction, it was the friction caused by modern government operating on populations not quite civilized in the political sense of that word. The difficulty will be made clear by taking an individual example. In 1844 there were almost 700,000 of a French population under British rule in Canada. French was the only language spoken by the vast majority of the inhabitants. Their ways, if dissimilar to those of modern France, were much more dissimilar to those of Britain. Their religion was Roman Catholicism, held with extreme tenacity and simplicity. They had leaders whom they trusted, and rights which they meant to defend. Lord Durham's *Report*, with its proposal to solve the race war by swamping the aliens in a British population, furnishes an admirable example of the obscurities into which nationality was plunging Victorian politicians, since even a man of genius, radical in temper and familiar with democratic ideas, could so entirely misread the facts which a special mission had made it his duty to investigate. Yet the policy of Lord Durham became also the policy of Great Britain until Lord Elgin began to modify it.

There was this peculiar feature in the situation, that British statesmen dared not, even if they had been willing, end their difficulties by granting independence to their alien races. In India, the absence of an alternative government forbade that solution ; in Africa, the presence of an overwhelming black population ; in Canada, the relation, geographically, of Quebec to the other British colonies. Whatever answer was to be given must be given within the ring-fence of the British Empire. The national or racial question within the Empire was really far more complex than the national question as Mazzini raised it for Europe. In the latter case it was mainly a question of securing sufficient diplomatic support before declaring the independence of the aspiring nationality. But a British proconsul in Elgin's time had to meet with all the obstructions and irritations which nationality could place in his way; he could watch the support which his country gave to new nations in Europe aggravating his own relations with his subjects; he had to work with nationalists who had been given the fullest rights as free British subjects, and the better and more prosperous his government, the more vigorous would be the life of the nationalist cause.

There were many other important issues raised by the development of the new empire, but these three were the outstanding difficulties, and none of the greater servants of the Queen, between 1837 and the end of the reign, failed to meet them in more or less aggravated form.

It may be freely admitted that, taken as a whole, British statesmanship faced its difficulties with wonderful success. None of the questions could be provided with perfect answers, for it is of the essence of a revolution that as its operations are uncontrollable by political reason, its difficulties find no simple or comprehensive answer; but if the empire changed no one could say that it was for the worse, and potentially the British state was far wiser and more powerful at the Queen's

death than it had been on her accession. Nevertheless the credit of the achievement has not always
been attributed to the men who did the work.
No doubt the Colonial Office functioned, under
its heads from James Stephen onwards, with most
commendable efficiency ; it cannot be blamed if
it failed to regulate the revolution. Most of the
Secretaries of State were wise enough to trust their
official guides, and three of them, Lord John
Russell, the third Earl Grey, and, later, Joseph
Chamberlain, devoted to the work powers which
are usually directed to more spectacular and
popular domestic affairs. But there has been
an undoubted inclination to speak as though
parliamentary politicians were the dominant factors
in directing a most complicated policy, and as
though the empire had developed through parliamentary commissions and eloquent orations.
Nothing, for example, could be unfairer to the
quiet, resolute, patient servants of Britain in the
Victorian colonies than to speak as though a
purely European figure like Benjamin Disraeli
was a pioneer and guide to the new empire. Disraeli contributed a notable idea in Indian government when he bade the Queen appeal to the natural
loyalty of her Indian subjects. He made at least
one startling and disastrous oration on imperial
unity, expressing opinions which, had they been

put in practice, would have flung the whole fabric into disorder. For the rest, he despaired on the very points on which optimism was necessary, and he never had patience enough to connect his fancies with the hard disillusionizing facts, which would have steadied, or perhaps have extinguished them. The qualities demanded by the occasion were very different from those of the old parliamentary hand, or the heaven-sent orator—less spectacular, far less adapted to catch the popular fancy, but solid as the hills, and terribly austere in the price they exacted from those who happened to possess them.

The British statesman whose lot delivered him over to colonial service, must, to begin with, have that capacity for scientific observation on the spot, which, in another sphere, made Charles Darwin the greatest British scientist of his time. A refusal to indulge in premature speculations, a patient study of all relevant facts, a conviction that field work, or, in political terms, service in the region to be reformed, was indispensable—these were the first requirements of the great pro-consul. The two outstanding examples of this power of inductive statesmanship are perhaps the Earl of Elgin and John Lawrence ; but there are scores of other names to prove that when imperial readjustments became necessary, they were made, not by cabinet ministers or orators in parliamentary debates, but by administrators who happened to know the complicated fundamental facts that mattered.

Pioneering administrators must possess that form of imagination and sympathy which we call good manners. This was peculiarly important in all matters involving nationalist cleavages, and race-alienation. It was so easy to fling back for a generation the amelioration of feeling which had been created by years of patient politeness. It might be the blind stupidity of an inexpert governor from Britain ; or the defective judgment of an ill-chosen viceroy, as when Lytton misread the politics of North-West India ; in half a dozen cases at least the empire suffered from the intolerable rudeness of irresponsible phrases conceived in the heat of a debate at Westminster. But the men who came to the front in times of imperial crises were all great gentlemen, and always won their victories as much by their manners as by their ideas. These manners varied with the circumstances of those towards whom they exhibited them. George Grey displayed his courtesy through his interest in and understanding of the Maori character ; Henry Lawrence and Herbert Edwardes through their sympathy with Sikh and border chiefs ; Bagot and Elgin in acknowledging that a man might be a French Canadian and yet none the less a very good gentleman and a faithful servant of the Queen. In every case it was a courtesy possible only to one who had lived much among the people he sought to serve, and who knew and loved their ways.

There was a primitive, not to say Mosaic, code of morals, without which the work of harnessing the revolution would have been impossible. Foremost in the imperial decalogue came honesty, or consistency, or honour, call it what name you please, whereby men might know that the thing spoken would in time be performed, the purpose indicated remain unchanged in spite of difficulties, all pledges be fulfilled, and no ugly facts evaded. It is hardly too much to say that government in Africa was simplified for all his successors because David Livingstone once promised to return from England and lead his servants back to the villages from which he recruited them, and kept his faith with them. It was essential too that the governors should possess a measure of purity of spirit—distinguished orators might have their pleasant vices, but regions beyond the islands demanded from their leaders a certain austerity, and Sydenham in Canada told with less than the power he really possessed, because men could weave scandal out of his private life. Simple kindliness had its place, as when James Abbot kept his pockets filled with sugar plums for little Indian villagers, or John Lawrence sat in the cool of the evenings, in grave and sympathetic conclave with his village chiefs. Moreover, as the beginning and end of imperial administration, there must be what Burke called imperial justice—the holding level of the balance and the meting out to each his proper fate.

In these early Victorian days it might also be said that a capacity for religion was part of the equipment of an imperial statesman. In the case of the great Anglo-Indians it took very definite form : and Livingstone, in his own way one of the greatest of Victorian imperialists, was of course a preacher of the Gospel. But with most of them, as, for example, in Lord Elgin's case, one has the feeling that the policy followed, and the more notable acts performed, owed their quality to a sense of responsibility based on a belief in a divine providence.

The mere cataloguing of necessary imperial virtues introduces an element of falsity, for the greater men possessed them quite unconsciously. Being instructed to act, and not to talk, they did their work unpretentiously and in the end confessed themselves unprofitable servants. Yet, if one were asked what finally determined that the state they served should persist and increase, the answer must be that it was the manly virtues of some great Englishmen which won the day.

The most notable group of men who served the Queen in imperial administration, as distinguished from parliamentary work, was composed of followers of Sir Robert Peel, and the period of their service may be placed between 1846 and 1863. It included two great Anglo-Indians, Dalhousie and Canning, Sidney Herbert whose co-operation with Florence Nightingale in army medical reform places him rather with the imperialists than with the parliamentarians, and the subject of this volume, James, Lord Elgin.

It was fit and proper that younger men who were about to devote themselves to a career of strenuous administrative life should have chosen to attach themselves to Sir Robert Feel, for of all nineteenth-century parliamentary leaders his was the mind and character which most closely resembled those of the men in whose hands the working control of the empire lay. Contemporary and recent critics have combined to describe Peel as a politician whose qualities, as conceived by them, never seem to give an adequate explanation of the great things he achieved, or the immense trust placed in him by the Queen, his colleagues and the whole country. Doubtless he exhibited few of those traits of character which picturesque historians and romantic readers regard as essential in their political heroes. Reserved in manner, sober in speech, lending himself not at all to the anecdotal inclinations of memoir writers, neither daring enough to be a radical, nor reactionary enough to win the admiration of unbending Tories, he has met with cold praise from all but those who knew him well enough to measure his true greatness. He was in actual fact the perfect type of the great administrator, and it was his fortune to train the best political minds of the younger generation in scientific administration. It was impossible for him to be, like Disraeli, a strong party man. He and his school had fallen on days when the solution of the most vital political questions was hindered, not helped, by ordinary party action. He had no doubt inherited a Tory creed, and it served to postpone for him the period for decisive action, so that he and the nation usually inclined to move together when events indicated that great reforms had become necessary. But, like all the dominating figures in the empire and in Europe at that time, he was a Liberal-Conservative. Never moving until his massive knowledge of the subject imposed on him an unchallengable policy ; refusing to resort to fancy and ingenuity when the situation called for scientific knowledge ; with the keenest sense of responsibility in his use of high office ; truthful and honourable enough to earn praise from the Duke of Wellington ; religious in the unobtrusive fashion which his countrymen appreciated far beyond any emotionalism or enthusiasm, he was a natural leader for men who were fated to spend their lives at work in which these qualities were indispensable. Of these lieutenants none, except the greatest, W. E. Gladstone, whose inclinations led him naturally to work at home and in parliament, responded more readily to the master's training, or exhibited his powers over a longer period and amid more varied surroundings than Lord Elgin.

The date of Elgin's birth, 1811, placed him among that notable generation of statesmen, writers, and scientists whose achievements shaped and gave its character to the Victorian era. He passed through the ordinary training of his class at Eton and Oxford, and, like Gladstone, his intellectual distinction was not confined to the examination schools. He took what they called the best first in classics of his year, and was elected to a Merton Fellowship ; but at the same time so good a judge as Gladstone said of his Union speeches : " I well remember placing him as to the natural gift of eloquence at the head of all those I knew either at Eton or at the University." [1]

His father's erratic interests had heavily embarrassed the estate, and in any case he was a younger

[1] Walrond, *Life of the Earl of Elgin*, p. 32.

son. So, with the sober resolution of a Scot whose fortune must depend on his own efforts, he lost little time in launching out on a public career. Defeated in 1837 in his own county, Fife, he entered Parliament as a follower of Peel in 1841, the year when that statesman began his historic administration. Under ordinary circumstances he would have become one of the group of Peelites who provided most of the intelligence and conscience in English politics through the next generation. At his election for Southampton he had proclaimed himself a Conservative who held to the creed defined in Peel's Tamworth manifesto :

" I am a Conservative," he had said, " not because I am adverse to improvement, not because I am unwilling to repair what is wasted, or to supply what is defective in the political fabric, but because I am satisfied that, in order to improve effectually, you must be resolved most religiously to preserve." [1]

It is probable that had his destiny been Westminster, and not the Seven Seas, he would have shared Gladstone's fortunes and joined his party.[2] But two events altered the direction of his life. His brother, Lord Bruce, had died in 1840 ; and now, on the threshold of a career in the House of

[1] Walrond, *op. cit.*, pp. 9–10.
[2] In 1855 he promised Palmerston a modified support, thus breaking, as other Peelites had done, with the official Tory party under Derby. *Hansard Parliamentary Debates*, 14 May, 1855.

Commons, his father's death not only cost him his seat in the lower house, but entirely excluded him from Parliament. As a Scottish peer he was ineligible as a commoner, and dependent for a place in the House of Lords on election by his Peers. For the moment he had lost his vocation as a legislator.

It was at this point that the offer of the governorship of Jamaica launched him on a career of imperial administration, and gave him a chance of grappling with questions as intricate and important as any in domestic politics, in a sphere of work in which he was singularly fitted to become a master. It is the object of the following chapters to trace the development of his powers, and the shaping of something like an imperial policy through his work in Jamaica, Canada, China and India.

There is something whimsically haphazard and casual in the fate which allots to distinguished men the work in which they are destined to earn distinction, unless indeed one is Calvinist enough to believe that events, or, in theological language, the decrees of Providence, are wiser than men. But when the young governor of Jamaica is viewed from the standpoint not of 1842 but of 1863, Lord Stanley's choice seems singularly just, and free from caprice. From first to last Lord Elgin displayed certain unvarying moral and political qualities which made failure impossible ; and notable as his record was to prove, the man was always more notable than his record. There are few whom it would be easier to damn with the faint praise of phrases like caution, tact, common-sense, and the like—imperfect descriptions of something which their users feel they ought to praise, but cannot quite understand. The categories of the historian tend to be too stereotyped. It is so easy to speak of the great orator, or the great legislator, or the great man of action. It was Lord Elgin's fortune, good or bad, to evade such short descriptive titles. He was orator enough to impress the politicians of the United States, but he never used speech as a thing in itself : it was always a mere means. He was so used to base his action on deep thought, and to strengthen what he did, as in Canada, by letting others think that they had done the work ; he was always so moderate, so averse from those sharp melodramatic crises which the crowd regards as signs of strong government, that few realized his immense practical power. More than any man of his day, except Peel, he analysed and tried to comprehend the elements of the situations which he was called on to control, and which, in consequence, he met with admirable coolness and impartiality. Partly

39

because of this, he developed an unusual power for meeting, conciliating, or, when necessary, quietly thwarting men who did not speak his language or accept his standards. He knew that Eton and Christchurch did not exhaust the permissible varieties of human nature. In Canada he was quick to discern the natural good breeding and conservatism of the French Canadians. He proved perhaps the most popular Englishman of his day in the United States, because he took the Americans as he found them. Even in India, his wider range of experience and the absence in him of the prejudiced provincialism, which so often calls itself imperial pride, must have done much, had he been longer spared, to modify the rigours of Anglo-Indian race prejudice.

His sense of justice was the deepest thing in him. To most men, justice means abstention and self-repression ; it inclines to be negative and artificial. But to Lord Elgin justice was ever, what liberty was to Milton, of the nature of things ; so that real prosperity must flow from it, as well as the mere consciousness of virtue. There was no pose in his mind, when he gave French Canadians their rights ; or prevented British traders from unjust exploitation of Chinese or Indian inexperience. Being quite normal, his mind regarded such fairness simply as the first condition of good government. But there were times when this mere normal justice came face to face with human greed, and brutality, and deception. Then justice in him became aggressive. " I have an instinct in me which loves righteousness and hates iniquity," he wrote to Lady Elgin from Tientsin in 1858, when confronted with Western misdoings among oriental peoples ; and indeed through his Chinese missions and his Indian viceroyalty his letters are punctuated with outbursts of offended justice. From first to last he never failed in his adherence to the simple creed of the great administrator—" to do justly, to love mercy and to walk humbly with God." So it was natural, at the end, that one great Anglo-Indian, writing to a friend even more distinguished, lamented " the termination of all the hopes entertained for India from his extensive and growing experience, and his love of what is honest and true." [1]

But it is more than time to turn to Jamaica, whither Lord Elgin, now married to the daughter of his life-long friend, C. L. Cumming Bruce, set out in April, 1842.

[1] D. F. McLeod to Herbert Edwardes, 8 November, 1863 : *Life of Sir Herbert Edwardes*, vol. II, p. 351.

CHAPTER II

APPRENTICESHIP IN JAMAICA,
1842-46

IN March, 1842, Lord Elgin was appointed Governor of Jamaica by Lord Stanley, the Secretary of State for the Colonies in Peel's administration, and in April he set out to take up his post. As we have seen, his position in politics was insecure, for the House of Commons was not open to him—and he could enter the House of Lords only through election. Whatever his motives, he was making a decision which shaped all his future career. Two lines of advance were open to him—British parliamentary life, and imperial administration ; and the more ambitious of his contemporaries, like Gladstone and Disraeli, had already taken the easier way to fame.

But, at the moment, thanks in a measure to Peel's preference for the positive and constructive side of politics, and his eye for capable administrators, a little group of men chose the harder, more thankless, and more glorious career of work in greater Britain. To these Elgin now joined himself, and the governorship was really an apprenticeship for a pro-consular career. Jamaica had occupied a prominent place in British eyes so long as emancipation was an unfinished work, and Sir Charles Metcalfe, Elgin's immediate predecessor, had gone thither and come away in a blaze of glory—he had reconciled a turbulent colonial assembly with the imperial parliament. But at last things had assumed a more normal aspect ; routine and ordinary administrative drudgery had resumed their sway, and an ambitious spirit was bound to look on Jamaica mainly as a preparation for weightier responsibilities.

He began his work in misadventure and sorrow. He and every member of the Governor's household suffered shipwreck, either in the *Medina* or in the *Iris* ; the birth of a daughter helped to undermine the health of Lady Elgin, already shaken in the shipwreck ; the nurse who was sent out from England in 1843 to attend wife and child landed from the steamer only to die before reaching the Governor's house. Then came the crowning disaster, for in the summer of 1843 Lady Elgin died after a prolonged illness and her husband was left, heartstricken, to face his duties alone. He laid the foundation of his

43

work in the death of his wife ; he was to complete it, in India, through his own.

To the aspiring administrator Jamaica in 1842 was chiefly notable for the problems which it presented—problems formidable because their causes and remedy depended on facts entirely beyond the control of the Governor.

Without assenting to Disraeli's judgment that " the history of the abolition of slavery by the English, and its consequences, would be a narrative of ignorance, injustice, blundering, waste and havoc, not easily paralleled in the history of mankind," one finds only too readily in the history of the West Indies evidence of the chief political vices of Great Britain, lack of foresight, and failure in continuity of policy. Slavery had vanished, and after it the apprenticeship system, and to them something very like ruin succeeded. Proprietors and agents, trained in a system as old and respectable as British colonization itself, found themselves face to face with a violent economic revolution for which they were hopelessly unprepared. England had paid the price of her sins in the cheapest way, a grant of money ; from the colonists, her fellow-sinners, she exacted the overthrow of their social and economic life. Not content with this, statesmen, both Whig and Tory, were now threatening to complete their work by

COUNTESS OF ELGIN AND KINCARDINE,
ELIZABETH MARY, DAUGHTER OF MAJOR C. L. CUMMING BRUCE, M.P
OF ROSEISLE AND DUNPHAIL, MORAYSHIRE.
DIED IN JAMAICA, 1843

abolishing the protection of colonial trade. Melbourne's government had fallen over a question of sugar duties ; but Peel showed every sign of carrying on the work of his opponents. For the West Indians, their ruin seemed all the more bitter because the threat to protection robbed them of all confidence in the future. Nothing illustrates so concretely the condition of things as a paragraph in one of Elgin's despatches on destitution in Jamaica.

" It will readily be believed," he told Stanley, " that among a class of persons thus circumstanced (the negroes), destitution can be but little known. It may be proper however, before concluding, to observe that classes more elevated in the social scale furnish a large proportion of the cases which call most loudly for the exercise of public and private charity. Of those persons whose property before emancipation consisted entirely or chiefly in a few slaves, many have fallen, since that event took place, from comparative affluence to the lowest depths of poverty. This class of sufferers, composed in great measure of females, are objects of much commiseration, and their support forms for the present a considerable burden on parochial and other funds."[1]

The Governor in Jamaica, then, had to face disorganized effort, poverty, and despair, among most of the proprietary class. When he turned to the negroes he was confronted with difficulties

[1] Elgin to Stanley, 5 June, 1842.

45

of a subtler and even more testing nature. On the whole the emancipated slaves had responded wonderfully to the call of freedom.

" The peaceful demeanour of the recently emancipated slaves," wrote Elgin at the end of his government, " their general deference for law, their respect for religious observances, have formed the theme of repeated and well-merited eulogy. No less remarkable and creditable to all classes is the rapidity with which feelings which tend to estrange slaves and slaveholders have yielded to the growth of more liberal and kindly sentiments." [1]

Nevertheless education into liberty is always a slow process, and some of its consequences in Jamaica were economically awkward. The slave, fresh from bondage and regarding field work as a remnant of bondage, was disinclined to work as a hired man. He had his provision grounds from which to feed himself and his family ; and beyond that his natural inclination was to become a peasant proprietor. Blest with a low standard of civilization in a country where it cost little effort to secure the means of living, he asserted his individual right to escape regular toil regardless of the general prosperity of the island. His position was terribly, or perhaps one should rather say grotesquely, natural, but the colony threatened to wreck itself on the rock of a disinclination to

[1] Elgin to W. E. Gladstone, 6 May, 1846.

46

work, except from hand to mouth, and except where the conditions of work could be modified to suit the new mood of indolent enjoyment.

Good-natured, too, as the freed slaves were, like children, and on most occasions obedient to law, they had the child's inconsequence and levity of action. Their crowd-psychology presented a variety of unexpected difficulties to their rulers. For example, it was their custom to hunt for crabs by torchlight and to trespass freely in the heat of the chase. Repression of such practices bred resentment, and when the assembly threatened to pass a trespass act, there was much probability that rioting and disorder would follow. Nothing but Elgin's good sense prevented the introduction of the measure. In the old days too, not without encouragement from their masters, they had celebrated the Christmas holidays in their own fashion, by noisy festivities in the dark—the act, 6 Will. IV, c. 32, which restrained them, contains many whimsical details about driving neglectfully and improperly, blowing horns, shells and other noisy instruments, and beating drums. But injudicious repression, no further back than in 1841, had produced rioting, and panic-mongers had prophesied a negro insurrection. Indeed among those barbaric children it is such absurdities, equally with real grievances, which produce general risings.

47

The negro religious world, too, offered its own risks and problems. Most of the coloured population professed one form or other of Christianity, but the attraction lay in hymn-singing, and some of the corybantic possibilities of sectarian ritual, rather than in simple religious truth. The new citizens of the empire were still close to African savagery, and if the Obeah man was not conspicuous in Jamaica, Myalism was, the other side of the Obeah picture,—the effort to chase Obi from the earth. In two parishes, St. James and Trelawney, the labourers " abandoned their work and devoted themselves entirely to the celebrations of the Myalist rites. The actual breaches of law of which these misguided people were guilty were chiefly confined to trespasses upon estates, committed in digging for Obi in places where it was said to be buried, and assaults on individuals, whom the Myalist leaders pronounced to be possessed of the Evil Spirit." [1] By impulse and training defiant of ordinary economic law, childish but with unexpected possibilities of frenzy, Christian by profession, but first cousins to the heathen of Africa, these strange souls had actually within their reach a great measure of political power, for emancipation was producing an increasing class of peasant proprietors.

[1] Elgin to Stanley, 10 June, 1843.

48

Here entered another problem for the Governor. The constitution which he administered was, as will be shown, very popular, and the franchise easily obtained. Now, as the history of the United States was to prove, the enfranchisement of the slaves presented a difficulty as acute as did their emancipation. At best they could gradually, and reluctantly, lay hold on political rights, claiming full citizenship only as growing intelligence taught them the advantages of possessing votes. The Baptist missionaries, however, had already begun to precipitate a crisis. These men had established, for reasons very much to their credit, an extraordinary influence over the negro population. They were tribunes of the dark people, quick to defend negro rights and liberties ; careless of and hostile to proprietary and " respectable " opinion. It was hard for them to keep balanced judgments in what they counted a struggle for righteousness ; as it was also hard for the planters to regard them as anything but traitors to white society. Sir Charles Metcalfe had declared with some unfairness that " the good that they have done would have been done without them, the evil is exclusively their own." [1] But certainly it was not prudent, not even Christian, to turn, as they did, philanthropy into politics, and to begin

[1] Kaye, *Life of Lord Metcalfe*, vol. II, p. 406.

a campaign, based on the rapid registering of negro voters, for the overthrow of the governing class, and the creation of a kind of Baptist oligarchy whose foundation would lie in the negro constituencies. In Elgin's first years the danger was all the greater because an initial impulse towards education had been checked, and the new electorate threatened to be quite illiterate.

The test questions, then, before the representative of Britain in Jamaica, any time after 1839, were these : the decay of Jamaican industry ; the despair and anger of the planters, and the strain on relations with Britain because of this despair and anger ; the risks and difficulties in the way of negro progress ; the melting away of hired labour ; and the possibility of the political predominance of colour. Besides all this, with 1841, 1844, and 1846 as special moments, the proposals to end imperial protection for West Indian sugar quickened the suspicions of the local assembly, and made the Governor's work of reconciliation and encouragement tenfold more difficult. Elgin's immediate predecessor, Sir Charles Metcalfe, had grappled with these difficulties between 1839 and 1841. Distinguished as few of his Anglo-Indian contemporaries were for justice towards those whom he had governed in India, and efficiency in his administration of East India Company affairs, he had been sent as Governor to Jamaica because Sir Lionel Smith and the assembly had disagreed ; because the assembly had refused to carry on the work of government ; and because, although England had talked of suspending the island constitution, it was felt that a policy of force would not really meet the situation. Metcalfe had exhibited, as he always did, qualities not merely of courage and justice, but of the most overwhelming generosity and friendliness. He had won over all classes, except perhaps the Baptist missionaries ; England once more appeared as a gracious benefactor, thanks to his open-handed benevolence ; and he left in a shower of complimentary addresses such as no West Indian Governor had known before. By a kind of counter-stroke of generosity he had answered these compliments with fresh gifts, and increased thereby the affection already cherished for him. As Elgin said, not without rueful humour, " the greater part of the addresses refer to the advent of a successor in the most gloomy and desponding terms."[1] It was for long counted the proper thing in Britain, with regard to Metcalfe's services, both in Jamaica and in Canada, to dwell on his wisdom and success, and to quote his example as a sure guide for aspiring colonial administrators. He had indeed done

[1] Elgin to Stanley, 6 July, 1843.

much, for he had prevented a crisis, by effecting a temporary reconciliation between England and Jamaica ; and such reconciliations, even while temporary, have a permanent value. Besides this, he had helped England by associating with her his own high qualities of magnanimity and generosity. But here, as, later, in Canada, he had not really grappled with the heart of the trouble ; for even when political problems are insoluble, wisdom lies in the frank acknowledgment that they are so. When he reported, at the end of 1841, that he thought his work was done, he must be judged a gallant and kindly spirit, crippled in judgment by sheer benevolence, by his approaching illness, and by a hunger for England not unnatural after nearly forty years of continuous imperial service. He was too willing to leave Jamaica with a premature *nunc dimittis* on his lips. The strife seemed over, the crown of laurels had been bestowed ; but in actual fact a final settlement had still to be won with efforts greater than the campaign itself had called forth.

Such was the miniature kingdom over which Lord Elgin came to rule in 1842, and such the benevolent despot whose uncomfortable successor he was to be.

There is little to be gained by narrating surface events of the years from 1842 to 1846, for they were mostly insignificant and of purely local interest. The Governor made an extended tour through Western Jamaica early in 1843. A little later, in August, a fire destroyed a considerable part of Kingston. There was a dissolution of the existing assembly and a general election in 1844, with Peel's sugar legislation of that year to act as an irritant to the nerves of colonial politicians. And so the humdrum record ran. A bishop died, and his successor was appointed; the island received the modern blessings of decent prison accommodation, a new lunatic asylum, a lazaretto, and a board of education; towards the end Indian coolie immigration began to relieve labour difficulties. The real history of these years lies rather in the social political and economical situation, and the methods by which the Governor attempted to modify evils, and create prosperity.

To begin with, he had to accommodate himself to one of the most remarkable constitutions within the British Empire.

" The means of influencing the course of legislature in this colony," he wrote to Stanley, " are of the most restricted kind. He (the Governor) exercises certain administrative functions in the presence of a popular representative body towards which he stands ostensibly in a relation of entire irresponsibility. In order to the maintenance of his constitutional position in its integrity, the acts which he performs in his executive capacity must be not only defensible but unquestioned. Moreover the powers with which this body is endowed are of a most extensive character. It claims the right of originating all legislative measures. It undertakes the discharge of certain duties which usually devolve on the executive. It votes the supplies from year to year. Its deliberations are not hampered by the presence of anyone to represent the Government or to speak its sentiments. The members who compose it are gathered together annually from distant parts of the colony, and meet, duly impressed with the importance of upholding their rights and privileges. Nor, be it remarked, are the movements of this somewhat curiously constructed political machine reduced to harmony by the accumulation in the hands of the Government of other and less direct sources of influence. Whatever power attaches to the disposal of extensive patronage, and the ability to confer important favours, accrues in this colony to the Bishop rather than the Governor, and must continue to do so as long as large funds are appropriated to Church purposes. The only influence to which, as it appears to me, he can under these circumstances safely aspire is that which may be derived from the confidence which the inhabitants repose in his attitude to the colony—his attention to measures— the soundness of his judgment as independent of personal and party feeling." [1]

As confidence in the Governor increased, the assembly entrusted him with new powers and means of influence. In his official report for 1845, he pointed out to Stanley a peculiar feature in many of the recent provincial acts :

[1] Elgin to Stanley, 5 August, 1845.

" A control over the sums voted for these services (public works) has been virtually given to the Governor, as in the case of the bills for the erection of a lunatic asylum, lazaretto, etc., by the introduction of a clause empowering him to nominate a certain number of the commissioners appointed to superintend their execution. An important principle, as it appears to me, is involved in the alteration of the practice which formerly obtained with respect to the composition of such boards, and it is not the less valuable that it was adopted by the assembly without solicitation on my part." [1]

He disallowed legislation with caution, and only, as in the trespass act already referred to, when he had a clear case of gain to public peace as his justification. At the same time he stood as a mediator between his assembly and the Imperial Parliament, especially in tariff matters.

How subtly and imperceptibly he used and increased his authority is best illustrated from the most notable political event in his government, the dissolution and election of 1844. His assembly was in its sixth year, and the question was whether it should be left to finish its course of seven years, or be dissolved out of hand. The arguments for instant action were many and sound. It struck him that the last session of an assembly, with the date of dissolution inexorably certain, would lead to a contentious session, members acting with an

[1] Elgin to Stanley, Report for 1844 ; dated 5 August, 1845.

eye on their constituencies. Dangerous propositions, too, for saving money were likely to be
popular, for economical reform is always the
politician's best friend before an election. But
the decisive argument for an election came with
the news of a daring new Baptist plan of campaign.
There was an Established Church in Jamaica,
reputedly cold, careless and conservative, with
social reputation and State grants ; and there were
the Baptist ministers, wholehearted advocates of
voluntaryism, popular leaders, and foes to all
existing interests but their own and those of their
coloured supporters. Given an election in the
spring of 1845, rather than in the autumn of 1844,
they meant to use the time in creating fresh constituencies of negroes, through whom the election
would be won. Then they would celebrate the
victory by ending the State Church. The first
move had been to organize petitions against the
Church from individual congregations. Then
came public meetings, at one of which a missionary
made " a very insolent and unchristian reference
to the Queen " ; [1] while a certain Mr. Knibb, not
without fame in his own day and circle, used strik-
ingly modern language about organizing strikes
of labourers, and announced his hopes of himself
entering the assembly next session. Elgin was

[1] Elgin to Stanley, 7 September, 1844.

always scrupulously fair to all factions, but he disliked the hot temper of the assault on the English
Church, and he knew that the Baptist propaganda
for coloured votes must prove harmful to all parties,
not least of all to the negroes, since the movement
meant the renewal of old mutual animosities
between white and dark.

He dissolved his House, and foiled their schemes.
In the election, the Baptist party took up the
challenge fiercely, the minister of Kingston engaging
in harangues to the crowd, and in bringing up
voters, while the *Baptist Herald* accused the Government of political fraud. The election was safe
for the friends of peace and moderation ; a
moderate assembly was assured for the next five
or six years ; and, to postpone the ecclesiastical
campaign, an act was passed, renewing for a period
of ten years " all the material provisions of the
Clergy Act which would have expired in 1847,
thus placing the establishment in a position of
greater security." [1]   It was characteristic of Elgin's
cool and balanced judgment that, in spite of
Baptist excesses, he did not disguise from himself
or his friends that the clergy must bestir themselves, if they were to maintain their position,
and that many of the moderates, while displeased
at Baptist schemes, would not be prepared to

[1] Elgin to Stanley, 14 January, 1846.

57

incur political martyrdom in defence of the State Church.[1]

Whatever view be taken of Elgin's policy, and of the Baptist attack, admiration cannot be withheld from one, who with few legal or indirect means of influence, could so unmistakably impose his will on all parties by judicious use of the power of dissolving parliament. As the later history of the assembly proved, the root of all the trouble lay in the custom of the constitution, and there was really little possibility of creating a juster balance within that constitution between executive and legislature. But it may safely be said that few young administrators could have used their weapons more subtly than Elgin, and that his temper, moderate, compromising, and far-seeing, was likely to prove helpful in dealing with the constitutional difficulties of the new empire.

Next in importance to relations with the assembly were those between Governor and Secretary of State for the Colonies. A comparison between the confidential letters to Lord Stanley from Jamaica and those written from Canada to Earl Grey, reveals not only the immense gain in power and vision on Elgin's side, but, even more, the cautious and official tone of his correspondence from Jamaica with Stanley. After all, Stanley was now a Cabinet

[1] Elgin to Stanley, 21 September, 1844.

Minister of senior standing, and Elgin was in his early thirties and still a novice. In any case, Stanley, who had not yet become, either in name or character, the Earl of Derby, was in these years an autocrat in his office, legislating with a dogmatic precision peculiarly his own, and claiming strict deference and obedience from his subordinates. Two incidents may serve to reveal a little of the individuality which the younger Governor was already developing.

Downing Street had, more than once, to ask for more information than had been received from Jamaica, in despatches and blue-books ; nor did the Colonial Secretary disguise his views on the point. But Elgin, who disliked, and continued to dislike, the use made of the correspondence of Governors by British politicians for scoring points in the party game, interposed a stubborn silence when that seemed judicious, being restrained, as he explained at length,

" partly by the anxiety which at this distance it is hardly possible not to feel, lest you should be misled by undue prominence being unintentionally given to circumstances, which a better acquaintance might prove of little moment. Casual indications of general or individual sentiment, which afford hints of much value to a person on the spot, who can view them in connection with surrounding facts, can seldom be safely transmitted across the Atlantic, and certain peculiarities in the racial condition of the Island when I arrived here, rendered it more than usually difficult to impart information of this description." [1]

To the end of the Jamaica chapter he never quite accepted home standards, as to the volume of correspondence expected from governors *in partibus*.

About the same time Secretary of State and Governor entered on an elaborate correspondence over a question of import duties. Among the tariff modifications introduced by the assembly to relieve land of its less bearable burdens, without causing a budget deficit, a substantial increase in duties had been voted on British, which in this case meant Irish, salt beef and pork. Irish importers had brought the matter to the notice of parliament, unfortunately before Stanley had received any explanatory despatch from Elgin. [2] Lord John Russell had said that the duties were " unheard of " ; and Stanley, fretted by Elgin's reluctance to write, adopted a very firm tone. In two convincing despatches the Governor, with minor surrenders, maintained his point, showing that the duties, old and new, on salt beef and pork, could not have been excessive, since consumption in Jamaica had increased parallel with the duties ; that the Irish market had languished even when protected by a preference of twenty-one shillings

[1] Elgin to Stanley, 6 July, 1843.
[2] Stanley to Elgin, 14 January, 1844.

and fivepence over American rivals : and that after inducing Jamaica to increase her expenditure especially on public works, as the Imperial Government had done through Metcalfe, the Colonial Secretary could hardly afford to disallow import duties for revenue purposes, simply because the indolence of Irish traders had let their market down. The episode concluded in a compromise, the assembly consenting to lay on a somewhat lighter impost. A weaker man would have embroiled himself with both sides ; Elgin retained their good-will.

That he gained in ease, independence, and humour, he proved by a little encounter not with his chief, but through him with officialdom with its innumerable and unintelligent forms—it was over a return to be made by stipendiary magistrates, and containing among its headings one entitled " Legislative and Executive Measures needed."

" Whether," he wrote in ironical circumlocution, " the interests of good government would be promoted by requiring public officers whose means of observation are necessarily limited, and who are as respects these matters irresponsible, to fill up a blank in each semi-annual report with suggestions for the guidance of the legislature, and executive authorities, is a point on which I think some doubt may reasonably be entertained." [1]

[1] Elgin to Stanley, 2 September, 1845

Trifling all these details may seem, but colonial government must always deal in such details ; and whatever Stanley may have thought of Elgin's firm stand over them, he had marked down the critic for promotion. The work in Jamaica convinced him that the government of Canada would not be too serious a responsibility for him to undertake.

So far Elgin has been exhibited, testing the instrument of government placed at his disposal. The picture must be completed with a record of things done.

For atmosphere and background one must imagine the sleepy, tropical life, in which not even rage against British legislation, and internal feuds, could stir men to vigorous action ; the gentle decay attending on the decline of planting and sugar-making ; the negro community irresponsibly happy in its new-found liberty, indolently defying what some call economic law, spending much time in childish sport and noisy holidays, with now and then flashes of fundamental barbarism ; the surface energies of the prophets of a righteousness which did not always distinguish carefully between the voice of God, and the political interests of a sect : and last but not least, for the Governor, the sense of loss and isolation which had come when Lady Elgin died, and which could not, in spite of all his efforts, but give the whole affair a tone of strain and unreality.

Into this island life came curious figures from the surrounding regions, to create a kind of minor diplomacy of the West Indies. Hayti in these days was suffering from a permanent epidemic of revolution and civil war—exhibiting, as Elgin put it, a miserable parody of European and American institutions without the spirit which animates either, the tinsel of French sentiment on the ground of negro ignorance. Out of this *terra incognita* came visitants of two kinds : one, gentlemen of doubtful nationality, who laid before the Governor of Jamaica suggestions that England might well take a benevolent, and possibly active, part in Haytian politics ; the other, deposed or retiring presidents, who desired a little rest and security before making their next venture. To the first Elgin invariably answered that he had no authority to interfere in the internal affairs of other countries : the others he soothed with good wishes and hopes that they might find in the island " the comfort and repose " which they sought. Cuba too was restless under her Spanish rulers, and once at least assurance had to be given that no aid in Jamaica was being prepared for Cuban insurgents. Then there were many minor troubles with Honduras, the Mosquito coast, and the surrounding republics, as their sources. A phantom ruler, Frederick, King of the Mosquito tribe, had died, and Elgin as representative of a nation which tried to combine philanthropic interest in the Indians, with a resolute policy of non-interference, found it difficult to teach the administrator in Honduras how to reconcile contradictory ideals in diplomacy. And in that age of incipient imperialism, there came to Kingston Belgians and Prussians, looking for commercial or political settlements on the mainland, but anxious first to find out how Britain would view their ventures. Apparently Frederick William IV of Prussia had, like the Great Elector, colonial ambitions, for at the end of 1844 Elgin reported the entertainment of a Prussian deputation interested in making a Prussian colony on the Mosquito shore. With their request for an opinion the Governor declined to comply, " alleging the two following reasons for my refusal : firstly, that I never spoke of business extra officially, or offered opinions on such matters otherwise than in writing ; and secondly, that I had no authority from Her Majesty's Government to deal with questions affecting the foreign relations of the Crown." Clearly Bismarck had not yet arisen to inspire Prussia with a proper sense of her world mission.

Apart from these more romantic figures and

ventures, there was, of course, the steadily increasing
pressure of the United States, but, happily for the
Governor of Jamaica, American commercial expansion had not developed into a new and powerful
diplomatic system, and the main troubles were
trifling personal affairs—American captains desiring
the arrest of deserting seamen, or deserving arrest
for luring Jamaican blacks into the slavery of the
Southern States. In all these things Elgin behaved
with the discretion which already was his most
marked characteristic : trifling in themselves, they
formed an excellent school for diplomatic action on
a larger scale.

The finance of the island was of course full of
difficulty in days when the planters found it hard
to meet old taxation—on land, for example—on
a basis of new poverty ; and when the Imperial
Government, just then feeling its way to a fuller
recognition of free trade, challenged any unsanc-
tioned innovation in the tariff of Jamaica. As
has already been seen, the Governor was more
or less ground between the lower millstone of
colonial independence and the upper one of imperial
control. It was vastly to his credit that he converted his inglorious position of buffer, into one of
real mediation in the interests of the local assembly.
Mention has already been made of the trouble
caused in 1842 and 1843 through new import

duties on British articles. The final despatch on that subject to Stanley is an excellent example of Elgin's way of maintaining the positions assumed by his government and of driving home one or two truths neglected at the Colonial Office :

" Looking to the existing state of the community, and the conditions from which it has recently emerged, I cannot doubt that the highest interests of the population at large, and the cause of civilization, may demand from time to time liberal application of the public funds to purposes of general utility, nor can I regard without apprehension the inconvenience and hazard which may arise from any material defalcation in the receipts, accruing from an import which falls lightly on those who are affected by it, and occasions neither heartburnings nor complaints in the collection. I trust that I may be permitted to request your Lordship's special attention to the following points. Firstly, the increase in the public expenditure of the island which has taken place of late years : the additional charges to which I now refer having been for the most part incurred under the administration of my benevolent and enlightened predecessor, in pursuance of instructions emanating from H.M. Government, and with a view to the moral and social improvement of the mass of the people. Secondly : the persevering and laudable efforts which have been made by the legislature of this colony during the same period, to support the credit of the Island by raising the revenue to the level of an increasing expenditure, and substituting a *bona fide* debt bearing interest for an issue of irredeemable paper, liable to progressive depreciation. Thirdly, the vast alteration in the distribution of the wealth of the community, which has been effected by recent changes, and

66

the consequent inability of the proprietary class to bear, as heretofore, the public burdens. And fourthly, the impolicy of attempting to raise an adequate revenue by any system of direct taxation which shall affect a large section of the population." [1]

Up to this point the Governor of Jamaica has been exhibited as a more or less acquiescent agent of the British Government hampered by external circumstances. But in one region, and that the most important of all, he abandoned caution and defined and developed a policy of his own, when he set himself to answer the question of the restoration of Jamaican industry and prosperity. What he did there is modified now, in our eyes, by the fresh disasters inflicted on the island when England adopted a free-trade policy. For a generation it did not seem to matter what Jamaica did : her fate lay on the knees of the gods at Downing Street, who directed their legislative providences with little care for colonial susceptibilities. But if Elgin's efforts were soon swallowed up in the new revolution, at least he gave Jamaica four years of rational hope that self-exertion might still retrieve the day.

The fact immediately in front of him was the ruin of old Jamaica by the emancipation of its slaves, and the deep despair which had descended on its

[1] Elgin to Stanley, 1 January, 1844.

governing class. What could be done to restore good spirits, and financial credit ? In one sense, everything which improved the condition of society helped, so that the overhauling of prisons, the civilizing of penitentiary life, and the quickened interest in the care for the insane, made for the increase of prosperity. It was something to be able to report the end of abuses ; even more that Elgin could say, before he left, that while up to 1845 the increase of crime had been progressive for some years, in that year at least a decrease was registered, and Kingston had the lightest criminal calendar in thirteen years. The opening of a railway between Kingston and Spanish Town was welcomed by him ; it afforded fresh oppor- tunities for colonial business, introduced new economies in transport labour. Immigration, too, was persistently discussed and experimented in even before 1846. Unremunerative attempts had been made to attract labourers from West Africa, and to fill up the gaps created by emancipation from the victims rescued by the British navy out of captured slave-ships ; but in 1845-6 the stream of coolie immigration from India began to make itself felt, as a more adequate solution to labour difficulties.

Elgin accepted and supported all these attempts at social amelioration. He saw more especially

that immigration was necessary to revive work on
the sugar estates : although immigration had its
other side, as in the case reported with a touch of
humour where " in a district to which a cargo of
Indian immigrants were lately conveyed, the
native peasantry received the strangers with much
kindness, observing that they were glad they were
come, as they would relieve them from work for
the estates, when they wished to cultivate their
own grounds ! " [1]

But the main object must be to dissuade from
that reliance on external aids which had done
so much to ruin industry. Self-reliance, practical
optimism, and energetic action, must be the watch-
words for the day. To achieve this Elgin steadily
preached the necessity of education. Looking
broadly at the situation, he saw the need for some
" bond of principle and sympathy to draw together
the friends of the negro and the planter ; and the
discovery of some common ground on which intelligent and conscientious men representing these
apparently conflicting interests might meet to
concert measures for the common good." [2]

Education, and reorganization on a basis of
practical education, were his suggestions. Living
in days when the Victorian intelligenzia, with

[1] Elgin to Stanley, 6 May, 1845.
[2] Elgin to Stanley, 5 August, 1845.

Macaulay as its prophet, interpreted education to mean books and theorizing, Elgin utterly distrusted contemporary usage. Like Napoleon he believed in training common men to think in concrete terms, and to develop themselves through taking interest in their necessary occupations. It was plain that the planters and their managers must learn the industrial methods of the new age : for, even before emancipation, they had fallen into the intellectual indolence which attends on all old-established businesses. Their equipment, mechanical and intellectual, was obsolete. Nothing could furnish a safer and quicker cure for their pessimism than mechanical and industrial experiment, and that meant rethinking out the industrial life of the island in modern terms. It was plain too that the cure for the masters would also be an aid to the peasantry. Where the negroes were not still drudging on with the tools and the methods handed down from slave days, they were abandoning regular labour, and gathering, in happy indolence, just sufficient produce from their provision grounds and small holdings to meet the most unambitious demands of existence. It was useless to make them read and write, if the end of the business was simply to produce a literate for an illiterate crowd of contented loungers. Industrial education would mean the separation between capable and incapable. It would breed an aristocracy of labour, capable of using the plough instead of the hoe, and understanding the economies of railway transport. It must be remembered that many of the alleviating features in modern West Indian life were not then in existence. American capital was still confined within the boundaries of the United States ; American tourists and their money had not appeared above the northern horizon ; the appetite of England for bananas and West Indian fruit had still to be created. The one plain and obvious duty of all true friends of the West Indies was to face with courage the gloomy facts of bankruptcy, and ruin, and negro disinclination to work, and to apply new methods and implements to save the situation. Throughout his career Lord Elgin betrayed a very marked interest in economic issues, and a startling capacity for using modern inventions and ideas to meet difficulties insoluble on old routine lines. It was in Jamaica that he first drafted the practical programme which he expanded and enforced in Canada and India.

Early in 1843 he offered a premium of one hundred pounds for the best practical treatise on the cultivation of the cane, with special reference to the adoption of mechanical aids and appliances to assist, or in lieu of, manual labour.

"Much," he wrote to Stanley, "is involved in the issue of this and similar experiments. So long as the island despairs, so long as the planter assumes that the cane can be cultivated, and sugar manufactured to profit only on the system adopted during slavery, so long as he looks to external aids (among which I class immigration) as his sole hope of salvation from ruin, with what feelings must he contemplate all earnest efforts to civilize the mass of the population ? Is education necessary to qualify the peasantry to carry on the rude field operations of slavery ? May not some persons even entertain the apprehension that it will indispose them to such pursuits. But let him, on the other hand, believe that by the substitution of more artificial methods for those hitherto employed, he may materially abridge the expense of raising his produce, and he cannot fail to perceive that an intelligent, well-educated labourer with something of a character to lose, and a reasonable ambition to stimulate him to exertion, is likely to prove an instrument more apt than the ignorant drudge, who differs from the slave only in being no longer amenable to personal restraint."[1]

One of his last letters on Jamaica, written indeed from Dunfermline after he had left Jamaica, gives a systematic exposition of his views for and practice in Jamaica. He had offered another prize for a treatise suitable for use as a text-book on agriculture in the island schools ; and in inviting Henry Stephens to assist him in the production of this work out of the three best essays, he indulged in a full statement of his educational aims :

[1] Elgin to Stanley, 8 November, 1843.

72

APPRENTICESHIP IN JAMAICA

" In endeavouring to introduce the industrial system into the schools in Jamaica, I was actuated chiefly by a desire to promote the following objects. Firstly, to impart a more practical and useful character to the instruction given in them, and to supply persons interested in the cause of education with an instrument which might be available for the purposes of moral discipline, and in the training of the young to habits of steadiness and order. Secondly, to redeem the pursuits of industry from the discredit which attached to them, when they were the avocation of none but slaves ; and to induce the planter to regard the labourer with feelings of increased kindliness and consideration. And, thirdly, to illustrate the connection subsisting between the material interests of the colonists generally, and the moral and intellectual advancement of the lower classes.

" For reasons which will be sufficiently obvious to all who are acquainted with the state of feeling which prevailed in our tropical colonies after emancipation, it was by no means easy to persuade the friends of education to adopt the industrial system in its completeness at once ; and it became therefore necessary to endeavour to prepare the public mind for its introduction by preliminary measures. The first step taken with this view was the offer of a prize for the best treatise on a system of industrial training suited to the colony. A considerable number of persons competed for this prize, and six of the best essays were published, and distributed gratuitously. In the next place, some very competent persons were induced to deliver lectures on subjects connected with agriculture in the principal town of the colony. The boys from all the schools were invited to attend ; an examination was held at the close of the course, and rewards given to those who showed the greatest proficiency. Lastly, in conjunction with the Royal Agricultural Society of Jamaica, I offered a prize for a text-book on agriculture for the use of the schools."[1]

His Baptist critics and their paper accused him, and the Board of Education which his assembly granted him in 1844, of attempting to prevent the peasantry from ever rising above the station in which emancipation had left them. But they misread his intentions. With many present-day educationists he believed that a race such as slavery had developed in Jamaica may be best educated through their natural and practical aptitudes ; and that it was not he, but the missionaries, who were reactionary in damning as degrading the whole region of agricultural labour for wages.

To the very end of his administration he continued his efforts. The Board of Education enabled the Government to give grants, irrespective of sect, to all who undertook educational work, and they exacted from their beneficiaries the right to inspect their schools. He strongly approved the project to provide adequate normal schools in which to train teachers, but held that there must be some element of practical and manual instruction in the course, in order that " the minds of all classes may be disabused of the impression that honest labour is in any wise inconsistent with the full exercise of

[1] Elgin to Henry Stephens, 4 December, 1846.

the privileges conferred by freedom." [1]   In his last
general report he ended on the educational note,
urging caution in the discussion of compulsory
education, but admitting that " if it should appear
that any considerable portion of the juvenile population are brought up as outcasts, in idleness, ignorance, and dissipation, the expediency of establishing
industrial seminaries, to which children so circumstanced may be consigned by authority, may become matter for grave deliberation." [2]

Except perhaps at the moment of his wife's
death, Elgin showed no sign, in letter or despatch
from Jamaica, that he was not entirely engrossed in
the work of his administration : but there can be
little doubt that his position strained him, and was
at times irksome. The death of his wife had not
merely been a crippling blow to him as an individual ; it had taken from him the support on
which he relied " for the discharge of those duties
towards the local society, which are not the least
important part of the functions of a Governor." [3]
It was already time to think of removing his little
daughter to a more suitable climate, and her grand-
parents were calling for her.   Like his predecessor,

[1] Elgin to the Rev. Mr. Miller, Mico Institution, 30 March,
1846.
[2] Elgin to W. E. Gladstone, 6 May, 1846.
[3] Elgin to Stanley, 7 April, 1845.

in the midst of his labours he had dreams of home, and in any case his private affairs demanded some attention. Besides, continuance in the government of Jamaica, " this remote and unregarded portion of the Empire," as he called it in a letter to Gladstone, was not a sufficient temptation for a young man, ambitious and conscious of his powers, and in 1845 he had filled this post longer than any of his predecessors since the Duke of Manchester. Even if he had no further views of great appointments, he had no intention of dropping out of politics, and a Scottish peer who missed his chance of election to the House of Lords might easily find himself without *locus standi* in British political life. Early in 1845, then, he made his first move towards recall, saying quite frankly to his chief that he viewed with much repugnance the prospect of an indefinitely prolonged sojourn in Jamaica.[1]

When Stanley in answer inquired his views about the governorship in Canada, Elgin was content to leave the matter entirely in his hands, only stipulating that, if he were to continue any time Governor in Jamaica, he would desire leave of absence in which to bring his child home, and disclaiming any particular ambition to hold a new government. In December he was definitively told that Canada was his for the taking. He was pre-

[1] Elgin to Stanley, 7 April, 1845.

paring for an early departure, when news came
that Peel's Government had fallen. Seemingly the
Canadian project had lapsed, although Stanley
promised to put on record the leave which had
been granted, in order that his successor in office
might act on it.[1] The arrival of his old school and
college friend, Gladstone, in the Colonial Office
presented no obstacle in the way, at least of his
project for leave of absence. He received fresh
permission in March, and sailed for England on
24 May, 1846, handing the government over to
Major-General Berkeley as his deputy.[2]

But events were travelling fast both for England
and for Lord Elgin. Gladstone followed Stanley
into retirement after a brief six months of office.
The Whigs entered on a new lease of office, and the
chance of preferment, even for a follower of the
moderate counsels of Peel, seemed negligible. But
Earl Grey, now Colonial Secretary, had obviously
learned from his predecessors the value of the
Governor of Jamaica ; and Elgin, who found on
his arrival that power was changing hands, and
whose dreams of advancement had begun to dissolve, was surprised when, on making his official
bow at the Colonial Office, he received flattering
offers from his new chief.

[1] Elgin to W. E. Gladstone, 21 February, 1846.
[2] Elgin to W. E. Gladstone, 22 May, 1846.

CHAPTER III

CANADA: POLITICAL AND CONSTITUTIONAL, 1847-54

THE interval between Lord Elgin's departure from Jamaica and the beginning of his next venture was an important period in his life. He came to England gloomy and out of spirits, to find his friends fallen from power, and the Whigs resuming their old control. The best, apparently, that he could hope for was permission to withdraw from his Governorship, and to try his luck in British politics. But no sooner was Earl Grey—better known in earlier politics as Lord Howick—safely settled in office, than he renewed Stanley's offer of the Canadian government, and on 6 August Elgin placed his services at the disposal of the new cabinet.[1] From the first he had no doubt that his new work would prove vastly more laborious and embarrassing than his old.[2] No sooner was he appointed than he sent his brother

[1] Elgin to Grey, 6 August, 1846.
[2] Elgin to Mrs. Cumming Bruce, 9 October, 1846.

78

to Canada to see how the land lay, and to free him when he should arrive from being a slave to his ignorance and his official instructions.

Events now began to move. He very quickly established intimate relations with his new chief. On his way north he wrote from Howick to prepare the Cumming Bruces, the parents of his first wife, and his life-long friends, for his engagement to Lady Mary Lambton, the eldest daughter of the Earl of Durham ; he was married on 7 November, and arranged to leave for Canada early in January, 1847—actually sailing on 5 January, for Halifax and Boston, and arranging for his wife and Elma, the little daughter of his first marriage, to follow when the weather grew milder.

For the eight years which ensued the life of Lord Elgin and the history of Canada are one ; in all the events of first-rate importance during these years he was chief actor, and, taken together, they constitute the most influential chapter, since 1763, in British North American history. Happily the historian of Lord Elgin's Canadian administration is absolved either from dealing with Canadian history *ab ovo*, or from writing a full history of the province from 1847 to 1854. Yet the Governor-General entered so intimately into the life of the place, and exercised so quietly masterful an influence on it, that his biography embraces everything of real importance which happened there. The impression created will be false if it suggests activity merely political or constitutional. It is possible to isolate, more or less, the merely political life of England at a time before social questions came to swamp its party programmes, but in a colony, early in the reign of Victoria, the proportion between the social and economic life of the place, and its political history, is altogether in favour of the common life. Parliament was an important but limited phase in the general progress of the people, and the events on which historians tend to dwell bear something like the same relation to real colonial history that the headings of newspaper bills do to what actually exists and matters.

From the details of the letters and despatches of that time there accumulates the overwhelming impression of a people, primitive, hard-working, at times fretful and unmannerly, but usually solid, quiet, and friendly, dwelling in great spaces where the forests have receded, but still maintain stout rear-guard actions, and where corn-fields begin to smile, and towns trim their rough edges, and mechanical inventions simplify the old difficult ways. The chief elements in the population were French, Irish, English, Scottish, and American, with their racial religions, Roman Catholicism, the Anglican Church, Presbyterianism and Methodism. Neither race nor religion must be judged by the crises they caused, nor the surface events which made men talk of them. There were racial antipathies, but apart from the horrors of the Irish immigration, especially in 1847, and the Irish restlessness in 1848, the masses of each constituent element lived very quietly and prosaically, worked hard to earn a living, and ate hearty meals in spite of all the rumours of bankruptcy and hostile tariffs, and the loss of British protection. There were religious disputes, but not greater than ecclesiastical perversions of Christianity have everywhere imposed on the ordinary wholesome religiousness of men and women. Schools and colleges were springing up ; municipal organization and the rule of law brought ever new order into the community ; and, if the intellectual life of the community were to be judged by the number of its newspapers, Canadians, especially of the Western province, were on their way to challenge British culture. In politics, thanks to Lord Durham's fatal decision to try to swamp French-Canadian nationality in British, the French had been forced to hold together in a racial political party, and although they were naturally conservative in Church and State, their allies in 1847 were still the Reformers of Western Canada, alongside of whom they had since 1838 resisted the attempts of the old colonial oligarchy, and the British bureaucrats, to prevent the people from controlling their own Government. The Reformers, whom Governors and Colonial Secretaries had combined to represent as dangerous and revolutionary separatists, were really, for the most part, very ordinary moderate souls, who wished peace on rational terms, in order that they might live comfortably and grow reasonably rich, and who talked much less about separating from Britain than did the politicians in London. It was not in their interests, whatever the politicians might think, to live among problems, questions, and crises. On the extreme left there were malcontents, who shaped their dyspeptic clamours into what they called reforming programmes, and, in French Canada, Papineau, who had learnt nothing and forgotten nothing since his futile rebellion, except some cheap and quite irrelevant French doctrines picked up in Paris, had now come home to vote against any Government which might offer itself. On the extreme right the old family-compact Tories still tried to persuade themselves that they alone were competent to govern, and deluded themselves with the idea that Imperial unity somehow depended on their monopoly of office ; and the Bishop of Toronto, who had plagued every Governor and Government since 1837 with his intrigues in favour of an ecclesiastical establishment now no

longer endurable, still persisted with dour Aber-
donian pugnacity in fighting the main body of
Canadian Protestants.

The situation might very easily be mishandled,
as Elgin's predecessor Lord Metcalfe had proved,
and the old cries of Responsible Government,
Clergy Reserves, United Empire or Separation,
Canada for Britain, or Quebec for the French,
furnished means of creating violent difficulties—
perhaps of ending British government in the province. But, even among the French, the trouble,
if it came, would be the work of blunderers from
Britain, rather than of Canadian malefactors : it
cannot be too strongly stated that nowhere in the
world did there exist a solider mass of acquiescence
and good-will, or a greater eagerness to obey anyone
from Britain who possessed knowledge, common
sense, and humanity.

The external relations of Elgin's new charge
were very simple. The connection between Canada
and the maritime provinces was of the slightest,
and promised to remain slight so long as the scheme
for an inter-colonial railway remained merely a
project—Elgin himself like Metcalfe had to approach
the provinces through the United States because
of travelling difficulties on British territory. There
was the British connection, complicated by the slow-
ness with which Downing Street read the plain

teaching of facts about local self-government, and now strained by Peel's substitution of free trade for protection, a change introduced entirely for the advantage of Britain, and ignoring, or explaining away in airy economic platitudes, the real disadvantages in which it had involved the colonies. That connection, however, was much less endangered than British politicians, or even Elgin thought. Whatever the situation now may be, the English and Scots in Canada in 1847, in spite of all the politicians, were unlikely to accept lightly a separation, not merely from their flag and their Queen, but from their friends and relatives at home. Racial homesickness played a greater part in empire building throughout the nineteenth century than books usually admit. As for the French, so long as their Church was secure, their nationality uninsulted, and their lives left quiet, they preferred *quieta non movere*.

The other external influence was that of the United States. The social and economic influences of the long common frontier, and the numerous lines of communication by water, made interchange of habits, and where tariffs permitted, of commodities, the most natural thing in the world. Population and money were being massed on the American side of the rivers and the lakes ; there was a common tongue, and traditions not so dissimilar. The question obviously presented itself whether continued separation between North and South was possible or desirable ; and while that subconscious strain of continental imperialism, which has for a century slowly but surely driven the Americans to expand at the expense of their neighbours, made every American an annexationist, commercial sorrows and tastes in common seemed to be urging Canada to yield. The old causes of friction over boundary disputes had for the time disappeared ; the border States had developed a more law-abiding fringe than in 1837 ; the border ruffians had in part gone West to seek gold. But there was the new Irish immigration on both sides of the frontier, and that pathetic effort at Irish independence which at home spluttered in 1848 into hopeless failure had a more serious counterpart especially in the state of New York. Half of Lord Elgin's troubles in the early years of his rule came from this source ; and Irish threats were seriously complicated by one of the worst faults displayed by the United States in her dealings with England last century—the willingness of the Union to play fast and loose with international obligations for the meanest political purposes.

" I have, alongside of me," he wrote in 1849, " a powerful people who acknowledge none of the restraints which international law and the comity of nations impose upon other peoples,"[1] and, later and more officially, " It is one of the admirable contrivances of the singularly complex system of the United States, that it secures to the citizens the privilege of molesting unoffending neighbours with absolute impunity, except when the said neighbours are sharp enough to catch them in the act. Given an executive at Washington which has an object to gain by winking, and any amount of war may be carried on, on private account, by the inhabitants of that country, without its being possible to fix the liability anywhere. I had some experience of this in 1848, and the beginning of 1849, when in the struggle of parties in the Union to secure the Irish vote for the presidential election, men and money had been collected in abundance for the purpose of striking a blow at England, Canada, although the quarrel was an Irish one, being the *corpus vile* on which the experiment was to be made, if only a spark of disaffection could have been kindled here."[2]

In all his work in North America, Elgin had to allow for this strong mixture of profound good humour, and unmannerly aggressiveness, of democracy and imperialism, of humanity and the meanest and most irresponsible vices of modern politics, and yet maintain a correct cordiality. As will be seen he solved the problem by passing through governmental follies to the golden common-sense of the individuals constituting the American people. Governments might behave like fools and knaves, but James Bruce the Scot found that his human

[1] Elgin to C. L. Cumming Bruce, 29 March, 1849.
[2] Elgin to Newcastle, 28 January, 1853.

counterparts in Massachusetts and New York were very like himself, and almost overwhelmingly good-natured and pliable.

It is too easy to impose an academic system and policy on what Elgin achieved ; after all his chief work was simply living like an honest man for eight years in Canada. Still his actions and correspondence throw certain aims and projects into unmistakable prominence.

To begin with, it was time to have done with the sophistication which had delayed the completion of Canadian local self-government. In spite of the eminent common wisdom of Durham's great report, Lord John Russell had complicated Lord Sydenham's admirable work between 1839 and 1841 by logic-chopping definitions of the responsibility of the Governor to himself and to no one else. Thereafter Metcalfe had spent his last heroic efforts in building up a Tory majority and ministry in obedience to Stanley's warnings against Liberals and Frenchmen. Happily for Elgin, Lord Grey had already laid down in an epoch-making despatch to Sir John Harvey that the most ordinary principles of British government by party cabinets applied also wherever Englishmen had taken up their residence in British communities overseas. Given a clear verdict from the Canadian people, expressed in a party majority in the local assembly ;

given also an executive formed on British cabinet lines, Elgin from the first saw, what any sensible great Englishman who lived on the spot could not but see, that the cabinet or Executive Council must correspond to the party strongest in the assembly, and could not but be responsible to it, however wiseacres in Downing Street might argue. He never doubted, or delayed, or argued. He wrote and acted as though, as indeed it was, responsible government were the only possible policy in a sane universe. That was the directing note of his policy from January, 1847, down to December, 1854. It is a confession humbling to our dignity and pretensions, that all the great discoveries in politics come from simple willingness to act in accordance with plain facts.

In the second place, he saw, what the few great Englishmen in each generation who are fit to govern others seem to be alone in their capacity for seeing, that, in governing any of the so-called alien peoples collected under Imperial control, not only is it absurd to bring an indictment against them for not being English, but that government of them on English lines is comparatively easy to any-one who takes the trouble to know them and to treat them with ordinary courtesy. For almost half a century the government in Whitehall had been struggling with the French Canadians, and as late as 1845 Stanley had instructed his Governor to treat them as traitors to the commonwealth. Within a year Elgin had seen that, treated with wisdom and justice, they were the most conservative factor in Canadian politics. This he knew because he had come to look at things, not through British eyes but from the standpoint of the French themselves. Almost the most characteristic action of these months was the invitation of the arch-rebel Papineau to dinner. " I found him," he wrote to Lady Elgin, " a very well-bred, intelligent man."[1]

He made two other obvious and therefore primary discoveries. It struck him at once that what in Canada they called political principles, and what temporarily were real springs of political action, proceeded from the refusal by the home government of natural political rights, or the imposition, as in the case of the Church establishment, of entirely unsuitable English institutions. When the grievances were withdrawn, the principles vanished. He saw further that, as an individual who has to make his bread by the sweat of his brow has little time for impracticable philosophies and problems, so a community with its land to clear and till, its roads to make, its canals and railways to construct, its children to educate, dare not waste time on mere factiousness and argument. Superior persons have

[1] Letters to Lady Elgin, 14 March, 1847.

damned the first essentials of life among growing communities by nicknaming essential material improvements as materialistic. As if all sound ideas did not flow from the careful study of plain natural wants. A later chapter will be devoted to the social and economic policy of these years. Suffice it at present to say that Elgin bade his colonists flourish in material matters by adapting their life to modern conditions, and so clear the way for such idealism or principles as God and nature meant to create. Linked with this emphasis on soundly material advances was the belief that for the province the most profitable party was one *of the centre*. With vexed questions solved and banished, there were not sufficient political planks to construct more than one party programme, and that was therefore really not partisan but national. Like Peel, and Cavour, and Bismarck, he worked for seven out of his eight years at building up assemblies and cabinets of moderate tone ; and this almost more than the concession of self-government was his chief gift to Canada. Ever since his time, except in pathological moments, the government of Canada has been either Liberal-Conservative or Conservative-Liberal. The history of Elgin's government is here peculiarly the history of the dominion in miniature.

All these rules of action received reinforcement

from the spirit which dominated their operation. Elgin sought peace in the spirit of peace. In Church and State, then as now, politicians and churchmen grew eloquent over *fighting* for their various good causes. The metaphors of public speech and action, borrowed from cruder ages, unconsciously influence us all towards a kind of political and religious militarism. It is bad form to think, speak, and act pacifically. Elgin had the good sense, or as his critics said, the bad form, to prefer ordinary peaceful methods even at the expense of heroics. He shut his eyes and ears to rudenesses ; evaded forcible methods of gaining easy victories ; suffered fools gladly, and always preferred carrying his point to damaging his opponents. This unique and original habit of his appears in all he did ; but he gave expression to it most admirably at the moment in 1849 when, insulted by his opponents, taunted with cowardice by the onlookers, and invited to a dazzling victory by his weaker instincts, he refused to avenge on the Montreal mob the harm they had intended to him.

"I have been told by Americans, ' We thought you were quite right ; but we could not understand why you did not shoot them down ! ' I do not, as you may suppose, often speak of these matters ; but this subject was alluded to the other day, by a person (now out of politics, but who knew what was going on at the time, one of our ablest men), and he said to me, ' Yes, I see it all now, you were right—a thousand times right—though I thought otherwise then. I own that I would have reduced Montreal to ashes before I would have endured half what you did ; and,' he added, ' I should have been justified, too.' ' Yes,' I answered, ' you would have been justified, because your course would have been perfectly defensible, but it would not have been the *best* course. Mine was a better one.' "[1]

The political events in which these characteristics were exemplified group themselves into three periods : 1847 to 1851, in which a reforming ministry was created and functioned under La Fontaine, and Baldwin ; 1851 to 1854, in which the Hincks-Morin cabinet worked on Liberal-Conservative lines ; and the last six months of 1854, when McNab's Conservative-Liberal coalition completed the labours of their predecessors, and Elgin assented to bills which practically cleared out of the way every question of any importance that had vexed Canadian politicians.

He had to deal with three main groups, developing later into five, and these it may be well to describe. First came the French-Canadian party under La Fontaine and Morin. They had been driven, by the attempt to effect Durham's suggestions, into a reforming party closely linked up with their friends and allies, the progressives of

[1] Elgin to Cumming Bruce, 21 June, 1851.

Upper Canada ; and under Metcalfe they had been stigmatized as traitors to the British connection. In self-protection they held together, and refused as individuals to accept appointments which would separate them from their group. Elgin found, in 1847, that it was impossible to move them from this position. He also found that, no sooner had he removed the cause of their fears, and dealt out to them the courtesy which they were well fitted to appreciate, they and their leader La Fontaine revealed at once the essential conservatism of the French-Canadian mind, and Elgin prophesied that coalition with the Conservative group, which, down to the death of Sir John Macdonald, continued to be one of the anchors of Canadian political stability. La Fontaine he greatly esteemed as " *facile princeps* among his fellow-countrymen in respect of power and influence," and he thought that if he were to reappear in politics after his resignation it would be as leader of a Conservative party.[1]

Later in the administration, more markedly after 1851, a little group of *Rouges* appeared, with Papineau as leader, and the two Dorions as able lieutenants. But as their views were too radical and too anti-clerical to suit their compatriots, they counted for little, especially under Elgin, beyond

[1] Elgin to Newcastle, 18 February, 1853.

helping to make a Liberal-Conservative coalition advisable.

The second main group was that of Upper Canadian Reformers, under Robert Baldwin and Francis Hincks. These were the two men who had fought every Governor from Sydenham to Cathcart on the issue of responsible government ; and the home Government held the gloomiest ideas as to the consequences of their victory. But as Elgin said, they corresponded very nearly to Lord John Russell, and the Whig section in England which carried moderate reforms. So long as Baldwin led them, they were not only the most conservative politicians in the province, but the most genuinely constitutional on British lines. Given the few essential reforms, they set their faces against all violent actions, defended the empire against Tory annexationists, and the Governor against upper-class assaults. They had, as their distinguishing feature, a respectability now known as Victorian, which proves how little their earlier critics had understood them. Of the two leaders, Baldwin stood for the steadiest moderate position then possible in Canada ; he was, as Elgin said, worth three regiments to the British connection, and, if he was not brilliant, his honour and integrity made him the most trusted statesman of the time. Hincks, on the other hand, whom the Governor-General always spoke of as the ablest man in Canada, and certainly the most expert in finance and commercial legislation, had more than a trace both of Irish brightness, and of Irish uncertainty. He was the natural product of a period when trade and money were beginning to count more than mere politics—just a little touched with the business politician's lack of delicacy on subtle points of political honour, but with the mobility, the alertness, and the freedom from prejudice—his enemies said principle—which made him an ideal founder of the new system of political conditions.

As the *Rouges* broke off from the main French body, so the Radicals, or Clear Grits as they were dubbed by one who later became their leader, broke off from the Upper Canadian Liberals. They were few in number, but not contemptible in influence ; for, after Francis Hincks took over the premiership, George Brown, the founder of the *Globe*, and once the chief editor of the Government press, flung himself headlong into opposition, and his newspaper made his action important. He and his friends wished for more rapid reform, and while he himself was above suspicion as a loyalist, others of the group were tainted with ideas drawn from American democracy and republicanism. So long as Brown led them, they were strongly anti-Romanist, a damning fact in a country where half the constituents were Roman Catholics, and they declared war to the knife against all ideas of supporting a religious endowment, or assisting sectarian education by Government grants.

Finally there were the Tories. The more notable of the old family compact had found the stars fighting against them, and they retired from active service, the ablest of them, John Beverley Robinson, being Chief Justice in Upper Canada. The fighting head in secular politics was Sir Allan McNab, a comic-relief figure in Canadian politics, although not without serious powers of doing mischief. He was bankrupt in fortune and reputation, but he had served his country in 1812 and 1837, and knew when to play the part of " gallant member." His intelligence and character were not strong enough to give him principles, but he had a boundless capacity for sheer personal spite and intrigues. He and some of his group were ready to do anything and join with anybody who could hurt the reformers in power, and Elgin who had placed them there. Latterly his interests were largely set on Western railway projects ; but the claims which long service and assiduous self-assertion always establish made it difficult for the moderate Conservatives to drop him. As for the moderates, they were of recent growth, and although they would have resented the idea, learned much from Elgin, whom they affected to hate. Their future depended much on the power of John A. Macdonald, a young Kingston lawyer, to win his spurs in high provincial politics. Under the Tory standard, as a kind of Protestant Jesuit society, rallied the Orange lodges, an organization so numerously supported that Elgin counted twenty-five in the Toronto district alone.

These were the pieces with which the new Governor-General had to play his game.

On his arrival Elgin found himself harnessed up with a ministry divided among themselves, and out of touch with popular feeling. Metcalfe, faithful to his instructions to concede nothing to reformers or French, had precipitated an election, in which he played the part of a sectional leader, with the British flag as dangerous party colours, and had won a Pyrrhic victory. Elgin tried to arrange some *modus vivendi* with the moderate French, with complete lack of success ; and when his first parliamentary session was held in June, 1847, majorities of 2, 4 and 6, all of them flattering to the ministry, showed that nothing could be done. The ablest of the ministers, Draper, sought security on the bench, and on Elgin's instructions a dissolution took place. In December the people of Canada were asked to vote on what was really the instrument of government under which they desired to live. Had they seen the correspondence of their Governor with Britain, their minds would have been vastly at ease.

97

From the outset he was prepared to give his ministers every constitutional support, but he told Grey that he was equally determined to do nothing to oppose the creation of a Liberal administration, if the representatives of the people so willed it. Indeed he counted it one of the most conservative elements in the system that there should be such changes of ministers. The one essential condition was that, however aggressive the Governor-General might be in non-party activity, he must preserve a position of complete neutrality in party contests. It was his opinion that the opposition would win by a small majority.[1]

After the session was over Elgin, who was now cheered by the presence of his wife and child, set off on a tour embracing all the most important towns in the West, Toronto, Kingston, Hamilton, St. Catherines, Niagara, and Brockville, and returned with two impressions strongly emphasized —the progress and prosperity of the British section of the province, and the appalling consequences of the flood of wretched Irish folk, which the famine had let loose on Canada; where Quebec and Montreal were threatened with hosts of sick paupers, carrying with them even to the remotest hamlets to which they penetrated their disease and pauperism.[2]

[1] Elgin to Grey, 27 March, 27 May, 28 June, 1847.
[2] From a despatch of October, 1847.

It was unfortunate for the reputation of the English Whigs that some of these tragic settlers were reported to have come from Lord Palmerston's estates, the more so, because, as the Colonial Secretary was able to report, the news was false—" they had been sent from the same part of the country by a person who is agent for other properties besides his."[1]

On 25 February, the new parliament met, and Lord Elgin was plunged in earnest into the midst of a great parliamentary experiment. The election left no doubt where the majority in the assembly would lie, and on 3 March an amendment to the speech from the throne was carried by an opposition vote of 54 to 20. The opposition leaders, La Fontaine and Baldwin, were approached, and, on 11 March, the first genuinely responsible ministry in Canada came into power. Although the Nova Scotian reformers had anticipated their Canadian allies in the achievement of self-government by some six weeks, the greater magnitude of Canadian issues, and the actual influence of Canadian example on the empire, have rightly set events in Montreal before events in Halifax as decisive in the history of imperial constitutional development.

The circumstances under which the venture was made magnified the audacity of the decision, and

[1] Grey to Elgin, 3 December, 1847.

promised either an unusual victory, or something
like disaster. To begin with, neither Elgin nor
Grey as yet completely understood the Canadian
party situation, more especially in its French aspect.
To them Papineau, and the attitude towards him
of the French Canadians, were uncertain factors.
In view of the subsequent insignificance of the arch-
agitator, it is strange to find Grey himself suggest-
ing that, even if the new ministry should include
Papineau, he " should not object, if his being included in the arrangement should be insisted upon
by the leaders of a party which can command a
majority."[1] For a few preliminary weeks, even
for Elgin, it was an act of faith ; critics would say a
leap in the dark. Such confidence was rendered
all the more difficult because, throughout the year,
the Irish immigrants in both the United States and
Canada were agitated by the troubles in Ireland,
and the American parties revealed themselves at
their very worst, in trying to catch Irish votes by
conniving at Irish American armed preparations
for a stroke at Canada. Rumour and reports
apparently well authenticated by British officials
in the United States suggested an imminent attack.
In September Elgin had thought out means of
resistance, for he considered it of the greatest
moment " that any invading force which presumes

[1] Grey to Elgin, 22 February, 1848.

to violate British territory should be promptly met, and effectually crushed."[1]

Still more threatening was the state of Europe, and even of England. Revolution, early in 1848, had spread everywhere through the continent, based both on racial and on constitutional grievances; and, what seemed most ominous for Canada, the centre was in France. Papineau, with his doctrinaire views, and his propagandist paper *L'Avenir*, seemed a natural and influential envoy of the new French revolution in Lower Canada.

It was perhaps fortunate that the assembly stood prorogued from 23 March; the Governor-General and his ministers were able to take counsel in quiet, and learn to know each other. In that moment when conciliation seemed essential, arrangements were made to give the French languages official recognition in parliament; an amnesty to all rebels still outside the law was proposed, and already a measure, of which more was to be heard, for compensating the population of Lower Canada for damage sustained during the Rebellion, was favoured especially by the French members of council. In addition, the Governor-General had now to begin to exercise his singular power of conciliation, and the actual opinions of provincial politicians had now become apparent.

[1] Elgin to Cumming Bruce, 7 September, 1848.

So far as the Reformers and the French were concerned, the crisis was already past. In a retrospect of the year, written in November, he reported to Grey :

" I have no hesitation in expressing my conviction that if I had failed in conveying to the leaders of the Liberal party here an impression of my perfect sincerity and fairness—if I had not (having thus prepared the ground) allowed constitutional principles to have full scope and play during the general election, we should by this hour either have been ignominiously expelled from Canada, or our relations with the United States would have been in a most precarious condition."[1]

The danger which actually threatened Canadian peace, although it was one of altogether lesser importance, lay in the attitude of the Tories, who now seemed definitely shut out from place and influence, and, as the next chapter will reveal, in the commercial depression which had in part been caused by the recent introduction of free trade in Britain.

It would be a mistake to suppose that McNab and the Tories felt deeply over any of the greater changes which the Reformers were about to introduce. They clung to the idea that they alone were fit to maintain imperial credit and connection in the province ; they resented the loss of patronage

[1] Elgin to Grey, 30 November, 1848.

GROUP TAKEN AT MONTREAL IN 1848.
THE EARL OF ELGIN WITH HIS SECOND WIFE,
MARY LOUISA, DAUGHTER OF 1st EARL OF DURHAM,
HER SISTER, LADY ALICE LAMBTON, AND LORD MARK KERR.

and profits ; and their resentment took the form
of intense feeling against Lord Elgin, the first
British Governor who had without reserve trusted
the French and the Reformers. Having no principles, but being steeped in personal animosity,
they were in a reckless mood, fit for all wild projects and foolish turbulence.

The story of their incredible folly in the " Rebellion Losses " incident has been told in half a score
of histories ; and its importance lies rather in its
consequences than in its mere details. But it
formed so exciting a chapter of Elgin's rule in
Canada that the mere outlines must be indicated.[1]

Immediately after the rebellion, preliminary
steps were taken, in both Upper and Lower Canada,
to compensate those whose property had been
damaged in the rebellion. In Lower Canada,
where the constitution had been suspended, this
was done by ordinance, and Sir John Colborne
with a soldier's disregard for forms had recognized
some £21,000 worth of claims, but nothing systematic or general had been done. In Upper Canada,
the process of compensation passed through several
phases. At first the legislature considered only
such losses as had been inflicted by rebels ; then

[1] I find nearly all accounts of the earlier history of legislative action about the Rebellion Losses incorrect or confused. The best account is in a pamphlet by Hincks.

the scope of the inquiry was extended to include all
military damage, whether by rebel action or in
official army operations. It was hoped that the
Imperial Government would help, but Lord John
Russell's refusal ended these hopes. The sum involved was estimated at £40,000, but while that
sum was accepted by parliament, no definite appropriation was made between 1838 and 1841 to satisfy
the claimants ; and Lord Sydenham, who hated
anything that savoured of a local job, ended the
project for the time on the score of economy. In
1843 the second act began, when a committee of
the assembly, with McNab and Sherwood, prominent loyalists, on it, was appointed " to ascertain what
plan can be devised to satisfy the claims of individuals for losses during the late rebellion and
invasion of Upper Canada."[1] That committee
never reported ; but the assembly in 1844–45
brought forward a measure for the payment of the
£40,000 already proposed to meet losses in Upper
Canada ; and, on the same day, introduced at the
instigation of the progressives, and accepted by the
Tories because they needed and were prepared
to pay for French votes, an address was adopted
unanimously praying the Governor-General " that
His Excellency would be pleased to cause proper

[1] Admirably stated in a letter of Francis Hincks, February,
1849, enclosed by Elgin to Grey, and also printed in Canada.

measures to be adopted in order to ensure to the inhabitants of that part of this province, formerly Lower Canada, indemnity for just losses by them sustained during the rebellion of 1837 and 1838." That address was accepted ; and commissioners were appointed, under separate conditions and differing from those appointed to pay to suitable Upper Canadian claimants the sum voted to meet their demands. These commissioners set to work, cut down claims amounting to £241,965 10s. 5d. to a more reasonable £100,000 ; then, possibly because French votes were not to be had by the Tory ministry, the business fell dormant—claims seemingly recognized, only to be forgotten ; and there La Fontaine and his colleagues found it, and determined to finish it off in the session of 1849.

Even in Britain, questions of pensions and compensation now and then take on an air of jobbery ; on the American continent they stink in just men's nostrils as centres of political corruption. Sydenham disliked the whole affair, and Elgin's own first impression was at best one of neutrality—" A questionable measure," he called it to Grey, in a letter of 4 January, 1849, " but one which the preceding administration rendered almost inevitable by certain proceedings adopted by them." The crux of the business was that the Tory assembly, which had voted the money for Upper Canada, voted also the

commission of inquiry for Lower Canada, probably
from the most doubtful of motives ; the Tory
ministry through its Provincial Secretary, Daly,
had ruled that, while rebels must not be compensated, only those whose actual sentences proved
them to be rebels were rebels ; so that, whatever
critics might say of the moral standard of the whole
affair, French losses still remained recognized, still
remained unpaid, and naturally were still held
fair legal ground for compensation. La Fontaine
was bound to listen to the complaints of his people,
and his Upper Canadian colleagues whose compatriots had been satisfied, and who were bound in
honour to La Fontaine, could not but support the
French leader. The Tories obviously stood bound
by their action of 1845. But what of the Governor-
General ?

Elgin was still *en vedette* on all Canadian political
issues. His present ministry was the only one
possible in the province, and it was treating the
question as one of confidence or no confidence.
Should he refuse his assent, not only was a Tory
Government unthinkable in view of the last election, but the Tories were actually the authors of
the existing trouble. Reckless propaganda was
tending to make the question a racial dispute, and
with Europe and the United States operating in
different ways to make rebellion and civil war

natural in Canada, Elgin could not but think that even a questionable measure was a cheap price to pay for provincial peace. Fortunately we have a free confession of his motives, written to his most intimate friend, Cumming Bruce, not in retrospect, but just after the crisis was over.

"You have discovered from the papers laid on the table of the House that this Indemnity Bill is not after all the atrocious measure which it has been represented to be ; and I hope that you will be more satisfied still that I have taken the right course respecting it, when you read my despatch which Lord Grey was to send to Parliament on the 25th ult. As to the Duke's saying that I ought not to have allowed the bill to be introduced, that is a very easy way of getting out of the difficulty. He does not know (and that is the great hardship which attaches to situations such as mine, such things never are seen or known) to what perils I should have exposed the Empire, if I had taken this step. If I had quarrelled with the Liberal party, when this measure was first talked of by my council, I am confident that I should have opened the gates of the province to 20,000 or 30,000 Irish American repealers, who were prevented from attacking Canada during the period of the canvas for the presidential election, while Polk was in power, and the jobbers of every party in the Union were toadying them for the sake of their votes, solely by *the circumstance that the Canadian repealers and French were contented and indisposed to rebel.*[1] Surely it would have been questionable policy to run this risk, in order to prevent ministers who were supported by a large parliamentary majority, from bringing in a measure,

---

[1] The emphasis is Elgin's.

which they had the means of showing was no new measure, but one which had already received something like the sanction of parliament and the preceding government. Besides, could I have formed a government from the opposition pledged to resist the Rebellion Losses Bill ? Would they not have said, ' We are committed to the principle of the measure, and the only way of getting us out of our difficulty and keeping us in office, is that Great Britain should furnish the money ? ' I might write for a week without stating all the hazards to which I should have been exposed, by refusing to allow La Fontaine to do what he thought his duty to his countrymen entitled him to do in this matter. Disaffection exists in many other countries as well as here ; but this is the only country in the world where rebellion is the resource always present to the minds of place-hunters—where to threaten the *ultima ratio* is not considered an impudence even, far less a crime. This peculiarity arises from the position which the colony occupies, relative to the States, and the tone which has been adopted of late years on both sides of the Atlantic in reference to agitation."[1]

The rest of the story may be told very briefly. On 25 April Lord Elgin in parliament assented to this, among other bills, preferring to assume all responsibility rather than allow Canadians to say that " the Queen " had disallowed a measure eagerly sought by a great majority of her provincial subjects. He was insulted by a Montreal crowd in which respectably dressed rioters were conspicuous ; and the same night, amidst other destruction, the

[1] Elgin to Cumming Bruce, 10 June, 1849.

parliament house, records, and library were deliber-
ately burned.   On 30 April, when he again entered
Montreal to receive from parliament an address
in support of his action, and condolence for the
insult, he was even more grossly insulted by the
mob, and his military secretary injured by a stone.
On 30 May, he refused to prorogue parliament
in person, delegating his authority to General
Rowan, because while he knew that he would be
adequately protected, he also knew that his presence would renew the rioting, and he had no desire
to achieve a reputation as a " strong man " at the
cost of bloodshed, lasting resentment between
parties, and very probably a race war in the city.
There was a recrudescence of trouble in August,
when the trial of rioters came on, and, in an assault
on the house of La Fontaine, a man of the mob was
shot dead.   By the end of October it was decided,
after very grave consideration, that Montreal should
cease to be the capital, and parliament was hence-
forth to meet in Toronto and Quebec alternately,
beginning in Toronto.

The consequences of all this turmoil were of
great importance to the Governor-General and to
Canada. The ministry and their supporters had
received the most unmistakable mark of their
Governor's confidence ; and the French could not
but appreciate his sincerity in recognizing them as

citizens in full of the commonwealth. None of
them ever forgot 1849. The Tories had hopelessly
discredited themselves, whether as patriots, politicians, or gentlemen. When the troubles were
at their height Wilson, a very moderate and admirable business man, later a cabinet minister,
approached Sir Allan McNab, telling him that he
ought to interfere to stop the excesses. The answer
of the Tory chief was " *If we don't make a disturbance
about this, we shall never get in.*"[1] Without a kind of
new birth, there could be no hope for a party whose
leaders were tainted with factiousness, so crude,
irresponsible, and brutal as this.

For Elgin it was an immense victory in disguise.
He had now behind him the great majority of
Canadian politicians. He was soon to receive
assurances of support from every side, and even to
the Western limits of his government ; although
the Tory municipality of Kingston chose to be
discreditably rude to him a little later, and although
the " Thistle " curling club of Montreal officially
excommunicated him by deposing him from the
place of Honorary President. But his conduct
reacted more deeply and subtly. He had incurred
charges of pusillanimity and cowardice by refusing
to take retaliatory measures, and by evading occasions on which his adversaries might put themselves

[1] Elgin to Cumming Bruce, 14 January, 1850.

still further in the wrong. He was thinking of the future and of the empire. He had to continue to live with—perhaps even to govern through—the men who had been behind the riots ; and it was desirable that no Canadian should be led to think himself outlawed from the British commonwealth. With immense courage, forethought, and shrewdness, Elgin made it possible for everybody to forget the nightmares of 1849, and so they remain unessential sensations in Canadian histories ; but there is still in Broomhall a stone, weighing two pounds, to testify that Lord Elgin had something to forgive and forget. It was characteristic of him, that when Lord Grey proposed to rehearse the events of 1849 in his book on colonial policy, it was Elgin's pen which modified the first draft, and prevented Canadians who had lost their manners and good sense from being reminded officially that they had once sinned.[1]

The worst was now over, but the malcontents had committed themselves too deeply to be able or willing to behave with ordinary sense. An artificial and quite futile British American League was formed, and met at Kingston in summer to express Tory *esprit de corps*, and pass pious resolutions ; and in October many of the political and commer-

[1] Elgin's criticism may still be read in a long letter to Grey, now in the possession of the Canadian archives.

cial leaders in Montreal, affected, as we shall see, by discontent with British free trade, drew up a portentous annexation manifesto. Elgin had an economic remedy for economic complaints. As politics, the thing was treason, and the representative of Queen Victoria proved that his complacence had limits by depriving all, who signed the document, of such official commissions or marks of honour as they possessed under the Government whose flag they were insulting.

Then, till the parliament met in May, 1850, Lord Elgin began to reap the fruits of pacific statesmanship. Preparatory to the removal of government to Toronto, in order to test the feeling of Upper Canada, he travelled through what was then Western Canada, receiving loyal addresses, and finding himself extraordinarily at home among the sturdy kindly farmers of Canada West. He travelled by land with one A.D.C. and a servant so as to contradict the idea that he required protection.[1] At Kingston there was a trivial discourtesy, since the Sheriff, and not the Mayor and council, presented the address, and a foolish Orangeman, who happened to be Mayor in London, tried in vain to put him wrong with the district, by sending in the address so late that a proper answer to it seemed impossible. " I wrote my reply in the carriage,"

[1] Elgin to Grey, 17 September, 1849.

chuckled Elgin, " and foiled him." Everywhere else not merely peace but enthusiasm reigned, and Toronto proved itself, Tory and Orange as it was in politics, both sound and loyal in sentiment and manners, and welcomed the Governor to the centre of its many activities. Not even annexation for commercial purposes could touch these honest Westerners, and Elgin had just pride in sending home a letter, written by Baldwin, the man whom the old regime had condemned as revolutionary, but whom Elgin knew to be the quietest moderate in Canada, giving his opinion as leader of the Western Liberals on separation or union with the States.

" It is due to my friends," he wrote to a political candidate, " that they should be made aware that upon this question there remains in my opinion no room for compromise. It is one of altogether too vital a character for that. All should know, therefore, that I can look upon those only who are for the continuance of that connection as political friends—those who are against it as political enemies."[1]

So with peaceful journeys, solid business, and some small courteous interchange of hospitalities with the Americans, 1849 passed into 1850, and once more it was time for the parliamentary session. Never did any delusion receive so complete

[1] Enclosed in a letter from Elgin to Grey, 11 October, 1849.

a refutation, as that session gave to the idea that the La Fontaine-Baldwin ministry was radical. It passed numerous and useful bills, some 145 in all, and welcomed such imperial reforms as the repeal of the navigation laws, and the creation of an independent provincial postal system. But on all vexed questions, and more especially on the two major ones of the secularization of the Clergy Reserves, and the abolition of seigniorial tenure in Quebec, where, on the whole, Canadian opinion had decided on the reforming side, the ministry, with Elgin behind them, preferred to incur the charge of indifference from their friends, rather than to ruffle the still uncertain temper of the opposition. What Walpole did for England, Elgin, La Fontaine, and Baldwin did in their smaller sphere at Toronto. No doubt George Brown and the opponents of the State Church resented their moderation, and moved somewhat farther to the left ; and in Quebec, the *Rouges* began to make their voices heard ; but there was general peace in the land. On 10 August, parliament stood prorogued, and on 16 August, Elgin wrote, with a note of autumnal rest in the lines, to Cumming Bruce :

" Our session has closed in an euthanasia. The last day was signalized by McNab's leaving his name in my book—a token that all enmities from that quarter are at an end ; and that the Conservatives think that at no remote date, they *may* perhaps be brought to believe that office under Lord Elgin is not such a bad thing after all ! A better feeling exists now between the French and English races in Canada ; and a better feeling (apart altogether from annexation) on the part of the United States towards Canada than has ever existed, I firmly believe, since 1760. Is it not something to have achieved this result at the very time when Canada is deprived of protection in the English market ? "[1]

Up to this point the dominating note in Lord Elgin's management of Canadian politics has been the establishment of responsible government in the colony ; and there, too often, the argument has been allowed to rest. But responsible government is rather an essential postulate of government than a positive programme and constructive policy. From 1850 down to 1854, the real object, apart from the passing of certain necessary measures, before both Governor and ministers was the creation of a Liberal-Conservative party and cabinet, which would free the country from its old factiousness, and unite all sound men in carrying on a moderate administration. Already, in August, 1850, Elgin had discerned the growing conservatism of the French. " Accident," he told Grey, " or, rather, I believe I should say, the artifices of Imperial policy, have connected them politically with the Liberals of Upper Canada. They are

[1] Elgin to Cumming Bruce, 16 August, 1850.

unwilling to break the connection, and they will adhere to it, so long as a Moderate-Liberal party exists in this section of the province. If Clear Gritism absorbs all hues of Upper Canadian liberalism, the French, unless some interference from without checks the natural current of events, will fall from them, and form an alliance with the Upper Canadian Tories."[1] In other words La Fontaine and his men were linked with Baldwin and the old reformers, partly by the memory of their old fighting alliance, perhaps even more through the real conservatism of the two leaders. Elgin always counted Baldwin the most conservative of all British Canadians, and in the late session, with regard both to the Clergy Reserves and to seigniorial tenure, La Fontaine had taken up the most moderate, not to say passive, of positions. Neither of the leaders could well head a party which did not nominally profess pure liberalism—they were guardians of a tradition, and they were both traditionists. But under them there were more accommodating politicians, Francis Hincks chief among them. Even in the earlier fighting days Hincks had been persuaded to join the eclectic administration which in the days of Sydenham and Bagot was counted more constitutional than a party group. As Inspector-General he was above all things financial in his

[1] Elgin to Grey, 2 August, 1850.

interests—the Inspector-General was the local chancellor of the exchequer—and financiers incline to know no party save that of sound finance.

He was interested in material developments in the colony, railways above all else, and material progress had not been well served in the past by faction fighting. He was too quick and shrewd to be beguiled by the war cries of the party mobs ; and he had difficulty in clinging to the prejudices which, with some other quite fine things, constituted what they called political principles. Elgin had immense confidence in him, and as some of the most important work ahead of him was economic rather than political, Hincks was the man marked out by him for promotion when the time should come. The chief interest in the politics of 1851 lies in the transference from the older Liberal to the new Liberal-Conservative standpoint. Circumstances removed both leaders. At the end of 1850 Elgin knew that La Fontaine meant to resign at the end of the next session ; and while he thought it a pity for one comparatively young to deprive parliament of the fruits of his experience, he knew that the man was not very robust, and that he hated the bickering and fret of party politics.[1] He resigned in October, 1851. But before that happened the other leader had gone. The parliament

[1] Elgin to Grey, 22 November, 1850.

of 1851 had been a disputatious one, and among the members from Upper Canada, the ultra section, assisted by William Lyon MacKenzie's worrying and fretful criticisms, and George Brown's whole-hearted Protestantism and voluntaryism, was making itself felt. Before the session ended, a chance concentration of votes had almost carried a motion of the old rebel MacKenzie to abolish the court of chancery, in reforming which Baldwin had done much good work. The motion failed only because the French stood fast by their old friend ; and Baldwin, sad because his Upper Canada supporters had failed him on what he counted a vote of non-confidence in himself, resigned, and persisted in his decision. Thus drifted out of politics one of the most admirable and wisely conservative figures in Canadian parliamentary history. So faded, rather than fell the first great cabinet in modern Canadian history. Hincks naturally took over the leadership in Upper Canada, and when La Fontaine went, Morin, whose views and experience were very similar to those of Hincks, succeeded among the French.

At this point, the fall of the Whig ministry at home, and the termination of Earl Grey's tenure of office as Colonial Secretary demand more than passing comment. From 1847 to 1852 there had been unbroken intimacy and confidence between

Imperial Minister and Canadian Governor; a most enlightening and ample private correspondence is the best memorial of the friendship. Grey had many other Colonial irons on the fire; he was a man inclined to doctrinaire views especially in free trade; he suffered, as compared with his friend, from seeing Canadian affairs through a glass darkly—he had not had personal experience of the difficulties which could only be solved by one who grappled with them on the spot. But he had an enlightened mind, an admirable sense of loyalty to his colleagues or subordinates, and a courage which Canadian affairs had tested, and proved unbending. He had sent Lord Elgin out to effect a great constitutional change, and even when Elgin demanded more concessions than Grey had perhaps been prepared for, he co-operated loyally in such extensions. Only on free trade theory and practice did he refuse to budge an inch—he was the perfect Cobdenite. He had defended his man against the very formidable onslaught which Gladstone and Brougham had directed against the Rebellion Losses Act. Now and then he thought that the Governor-General of Canada was a little sparing in official despatches, (of letters he could not complain), but when Elgin protested against sending anything over to Britain, in times of crisis, which might be used on either side of the Atlantic for mere party purposes, he acquiesced. When Elgin suggested that the Colonial Office might soon expect him to come home, Grey wrote an answer which was in every line of it an unusual compliment :

" You need not expect from *me*, while I continue in office, any intimation that your term of government is expired, and your successor going to be appointed. I should have too much difficulty in replacing you, not to wish you to remain where you are as long as you can ; and I should be much inclined to think that for your sake, as well as for the public interest, it would be desirable that you should stay at least a little beyond the usual time, in order that the good results of what I may call our policy may be more fully apparent. I have great confidence in the growing prosperity of Canada under the present system of government, and of commercial policy ; and if we could but set going the construction of the great North American railway before we cease to have the management of its concerns, I think we might fairly claim some credit for what we have accomplished."[1]

As a matter of fact Grey was the first to go ; and the parting words which the man who introduced in practice our modern system of dominion government wrote to the Secretary of State for the Colonies who had faith enough to trust him as he introduced it, must be given in full.

" I need hardly say that the intimation conveyed to me in your letter of the 26th ult. that you are writing to

[1] Grey to Elgin, 11 August, 1851.

me from the Colonial Office for the last time is received by me with the liveliest regret, although you may not think it one which calls for condolence as respects yourself. Having had the satisfaction of serving under you for upwards of five years, during the whole of which period I have been permitted to keep up such constant and familiar communication with you as has enabled me at once clearly to appreciate your views and sentiments, and fully to expound my own, and having moreover at all times received from you the most frank and generous support, it is difficult at first to realize the fact that this official relationship has absolutely come to an end. . . . You have good reason to congratulate yourself on the position in which, in retiring from office, you leave affairs in British North America. You have placed the relation between the Mother Country and the provinces on a footing which *may* (I do not say *must* for *l'homme propose mais Dieu dispose*, and I know that accident or error may militate against us) secure their permanency. And you have rendered it highly improbable that we shall ever quarrel seriously with our Yankee neighbours on a Canadian question. For although the lust of dominion may tempt them to grasp at the province, they are obliged to admit that the principles of self-government are established here, and they can no longer veil their ambition with pretext of intervention on behalf of the oppressed. These are great services. Nevertheless it may be doubtful whether they will ever be fittingly acknowledged. It is impossible to please those who do not know their own minds ; and until the people of England have settled whether they wish to keep the Colonies or to lose them, little credit will be gained by those who make efforts to preserve them."[1]

---

[1] Elgin to Grey, 19 March, 1852.

Between 1851 and 1853 two series of events seriously influenced Lord Elgin's policy, one Canadian, the other, changes in British politics.

The question of the Clergy Reserves had been down to 1840 what Elgin called " That regular old *cheval de bataille* of the Upper Canadian legislature." The Act of 1791 had projected a scheme of Church establishment in ambiguous terms, furnishing an endowment through land concessions equal to one-seventh of all land grants made in the colony.[1] The Anglican Church had appropriated the whole concession to itself, until a legal decision had made way for the Scottish Church to a portion. The growth of Methodism, the identification of the Clergy Reserve endowment with the old family compact clique, and the uncompromising and persistent policy of Dr. Strachan, now Bishop of Toronto, had made this project of a Protestant Canadian Establishment one of the major grievances of the reformers, and to Lord Sydenham it had seemed one of the main causes of the rebellion. Sydenham had induced the Imperial Government to settle the question by compromise in an Imperial Act of 1840, although the influence of the English

---

[1] It is high time that Canadian historians should cease to speak of the grant proposed as one-seventh of all land granted. It was to be an amount equal to one-seventh of the land granted—that is actually one-eighth of the total amount.

bishops had modified Sydenham's original plan in favour of the Anglicans. There the thing halted for some years. But before and during 1850 agitation revived for a variety of reasons. Under Metcalfe's emergency Government the Tory Anglicans had attempted to improve the position of their Church, and the strenuous campaign which the Bishop of Toronto was now conducting to create an Anglican university for the province, in competition with the " godless " college which the government had now established at Toronto, proved a strong stimulant to an opposition which had really only been slumbering. It was an unfortunate moment in which to disturb the public mind. The whole question of Church and State had been violently agitated by the Free Church movement and the Disruption of the Church in Scotland ; and George Brown, Scotsman in all his views and prejudices, and born to the work of effective political agitation, was now on the warpath, to free religion from connection with the State, and incidentally to deal as many shrewd knocks as he could at episcopacy, and, at one remove, at Romanism. Stripped of all its accidents, the question was really one of the right of the province to control itself in Church affairs as in temporalities, and to assume complete control over the very considerable endowment which at present seemed to be under non-democratic management. On the whole the solid mass of Upper Canadian opinion was moving towards a policy of secularization. Elgin's own inclination was for tranquillity and a passive policy, if that were possible. He disliked violent argumentative issues, and in George Brown's hands, the Clergy Reserves were rapidly taking the place of Responsible Government as a political war-cry. In Brown's hands, too, the agitation was threatening to involve Roman Catholicism in the fight, for Brown, like Lord John Russell, had a keen scent for Papal encroachments. With any encouragement a fresh purely political split might occur ranging the British Protestant Reformers on one side, and the French Canadians in unnatural alliance with the Bishop of Toronto's Tory friends on the other ; and Elgin's ambition was to keep the French from decided action as a racial party, and to lead the province away from questions whose exciting power was out of all proportion to their real importance. His two chief ministers, Baldwin and La Fontaine, were entirely at one with him here. Baldwin, although a devout Anglican, always held that the State endowment was a weakness to his Church, but he would have preferred, for the sake of peace, to maintain the compromise of 1840, had this been possible. La Fontaine, with his French Canadian conservatism, believed in defending legal vested interests ; his ecclesiastical sympathies set him against a policy of secularization ; and in any case, he held it to be invidious for French Roman Catholics to take part in an agitation for depriving British Protestant Churchmen of their religious endowments. But both men were resolute believers in self-government, and they knew that the majority of the cabinet, and the majority of the British Canadian population wished, in the first place, to be freed from the shackles of the Imperial Act, and in the second place to secularize the reserves. In the session of 1850 an address was voted, praying Her Majesty to obtain the repeal of the Imperial Act passed in 1840, and to hand over the Clergy Reserves to the Canadian parliament ; and Elgin, in a private letter to Grey, warned him in grave terms :

"I must candidly say I very much doubt whether you will be able to preserve the Colony if you retain it on the statute book. Even La Fontaine and others who recognize certain vested rights of the Protestant churches, under the constitution act of 1840, advocate the repeal of the Imperial Act of 1840, firstly because Lower Canada was not consulted at all when it was passed, and secondly because the distribution made under that act is an unfair one."[1]

From that point he never really varied, urging the necessity of allowing the colonists to settle what

[1] Elgin to Grey, 5 July, 1850.

was a local affair for themselves. The only doubtful point for him was whether he could induce his people either to make a moderate and compromising settlement of the fund, or so to secularize it that party feeling on the subject might for ever cease to create friction. So long as Grey remained at the Colonial Office, Downing Street met him much more than half way. Grey had objected to the 1840 measure, and had abstained from opposing it only because he understood that the leaders of both British parties had agreed to give Sydenham a moderate compromise to bring peace in Canada.[1]

" I am bound to say," he wrote on 2 October, 1850, " that substantially I think the Colonial legislature justified in their objection to the existing arrangement, and that parliament ought to remove the obstacle to their dealing with the subject as they may think proper."[2]

The only cause for delay in Britain was first that in 1850 and 1851 Russell was involved in his foolish Roman aggressions agitation which took up all available time in parliament ; and in 1851, with a wavering House of Commons unable to speak with decisive authority, and a Tory House of Lords, there was every chance that colonial desires would be rudely checked by an adverse vote in the Upper House. In February, 1852, the Whig Government

[1] Grey to Elgin, 26 July, 1850.
[2] Grey to Elgin, 2 October, 1850.

fell, and the friends of the Bishop of Toronto reigned
in Downing Street. It would serve no good purpose to give the history of the abolition of the fund
in detail. Suffice it to say that after the measure
had been held up throughout 1852 in England, the
Aberdeen ministry left the colonists free to do as
they liked in 1853; there was a slight delay in
Canada; but the secularization was effected by the
Coalition ministry at the end of 1854.

Not only did the whole affair immensely embar-
rass the Governor-General; but it shook the
solidarity of the Upper Canadian section of his
government; it bred factious agitation; and by
undermining public confidence in Francis Hincks,
it brought about a ministerial crisis in June, 1854.

The second cause of trouble between 1851 and
1853 was the change of government in Britain in
February, 1852, and the troubled and troubling
Derby-Disraeli administration which struggled
along between February and December. It provided the one grave risk of failure which Elgin ran
between his arrival and his departure. The new
government not only threatened to be reactionary;
but, with Disraeli guiding its councils, it was in-
sincerely reactionary and therefore incalculable in
its operations.

The appointment of the new Colonial Secretary
is best and most vividly described in a memoran-

dum by Disraeli himself. There had been some difficulty in finding a man, and Derby was in distress. At this point Disraeli intervened.

> " ' I know the man,' I said, ' he will do very well.'
> " ' Who ? '
> " ' Pakington ! '
> " ' I have just sent for him to be Under Secretary to Walpole. It should be a country gentleman. I thought it was a capital arrangement. He will be here in a few minutes.'
> " Sir John Pakington was announced. He remained in the waiting-room, while I was convincing Lord Derby that he would make a competent Secretary of State. It was, naturally, rather hard work. I don't know that Lord Derby had even a personal acquaintance with Pakington at that moment. The exigency at last conquered him ; he said, with an almost merry face of perplexity : ' Will you be bail for him ? '
> " ' To any amount,' I said.
> " I had only a public acquaintance with Pakington, who though obliged to vote with the Protectionists, always kept aloof, and fetched up with the Peelites, for which Peel made him a Baronet. But I had observed him, especially on Lord George Bentinck's colonial committee."[1]

In this fashion the founder of modern imperialism proposed to give Elgin a chief who would be competent to co-operate with him in working the new constitutional machine on which the fortunes of the empire definitely depended.

[1] Monypenny and Buckle, *Life of Disraeli*, Vol. III, pp. 344-5.

It is possible, by reading between the lines of Elgin's letters to Cumming Bruce, who was on the Board of Control in the new government, to see how perilous Elgin's position now was. The colony had definitely asked to be released from an embarrassing imperial statute ; but the Church party was now in office, and the views of the Bishop of Toronto actually outweighed, with them, the solid vote of the provincial administration, and the definite advice of the Governor-General. The British cabinet was strongly Tory, and they seem to have resented Elgin's introduction to them of Francis Hincks, as the request to recognize a dangerous and violent politician. It was late in October before Pakington invited Elgin to write confidentially to him on the affairs of the most important colony under his supervision, and his answer to some admirably moderate statements on the state of affairs in Canada was to draft a despatch, which refused the provincial request for freedom to settle their own ecclesiastical affairs. By one of those fortunate accidents, which have so often saved the empire from the folly of its supporters, the government fell before the despatch could be sent ; but by laying it before parliament early in 1853 Pakington did his best to make a crisis in the colony. It seems clear that the continuance of Elgin in control was seriously discussed ; for, as Elgin pointed out to his friend Cumming Bruce, in October, *The Times*, while it did not confirm a floating rumour of re-call, stated that the " rumour was at least premature."[1] Still, in the midst of his best constructive work in Canada, governing with a moderation and conservatism beyond all praise, and convinced that a change of policy might have catastrophic results, Elgin laid his views before Cumming Bruce with all the emphasis at his disposal, plainly expecting his friend to pass on his sentiments to his colleagues :

" I send a paragraph from a conservative paper of Montreal, containing a report which is very generally believed here. If it be true that Lord Desart made the confidence in question to the writer of the letter, before any communication to the same effect has been addressed to me, I think he has shown a lack both of courtesy and discretion. As respects the matter of the report, I am disposed to believe that, viewing the question with reference to personal interests exclusively, my removal from hence would not be any disadvantage to me. The only doubt that would arise on that head would be as to whether, if I am about to be discourteously removed, that is to say removed in such a manner as to signify that Her Majesty's present advisers attach no special value to my services, I should not have acted more prudently if I had anticipated their proceeding by tendering my resignation, as I proposed to do some time ago.

" But as to my work here, there is the rub. Is it to be

---

[1] Elgin to Cumming Bruce, 2 October, 1852.

all undone ? I have been possessed (I use the word advisedly for I fear that most persons in England still consider it a case of *possession*) with the idea that it is possible to maintain on the soil of British America, and in the face of republican America, British institutions, if you give the latter freely and trustingly. Faith where it is sincere is always catching, and I have imparted this faith more or less thoroughly to all Canadian statesmen with whom I have been in official relationship since 1848, and to all intelligent Englishmen with whom I have come in contact since 1850, as witness Lord Wharncliffe, Waldegrave, Tremenhere, etc.

" Now if the Governor ceases to possess this faith, or to have the faculty of imparting it, I confess I fear that ere long it will become extinct in other breasts likewise. I believe that it is equally an error to imagine with one old-fashioned party that you can govern such dependencies as this on the antiquated bureaucratic principle, by means of rescripts from Downing Street in defiance of the popular legislatures, and on the hypothesis that one local faction monopolizes all the loyalty of the colony ; and to suppose with the radical or Gladstone men that all is done when you have simply told the colonists to ' Go to the Devil their own way.' I believe on the contrary that there is more room for the exercise of influence on the part of the Governor under my system than under any that ever was before devised—an influence however wholly moral, an influence of suasion, sympathy, and moderation, which softens the temper, while it elevates the aims of local politics. It is of course altogether impossible to furnish evidence of the facts. If the thing could be tested I should be perfectly willing to rest the defence of my system of administration on the establishment of the proposition that the Governor-General of Canada never exercised a more powerful influence in the councils of the colony than he does at the present moment."[1]

Meanwhile, in spite of cross currents in England, Elgin proceeded with his reconstruction of the Canadian Government on a Conservative-Liberal and non-controversial basis. Hincks and Morin now occupied the positions which Baldwin and La Fontaine had held, and the election at the end of 1851 provided them with a substantial majority. The evolution of " Ultra " groups in both Upper and Lower Canada had made it important to strengthen the centre, and there can be no doubt that Elgin foresaw, as the constituent elements of that centre, the main body of the French, the moderate reformers from the West, and the younger body of Conservatives who were now beginning to look past Sir Allan McNab, to the more reasonable and accommodating leadership of John A. Macdonald. For the present, the Tories were left out of the arrangement. The Hincks-Morin ministry made a bid for Western radical support by taking in two of the " Clear Grit " men, Rolph and Cameron—without much advantage to themselves, as it proved. Along with the creation of this

[1] Elgin to Cumming Bruce, 18 September, 1852. Lord Elgin's correspondence, in this year, with Mr. Cumming Bruce, reveals how precarious the Governor-General was finding his position during Derby's administration.

moderate party Elgin and Hincks planned a series of measures which would lift the province from the atmosphere of argumentation into which the ultras were trying to drive it down, and give politics a positive and constructive character. The parliamentary session of 1852–53, which was divided into two parts by an adjournment from 10 November, 1852, to 14 February, 1853, was filled with measures of this description. Hincks had met with a double rebuff on his visit to England in 1852. Derby and Pakington would have nothing to do either with his railway project, or with Clergy Reserve reform. Elgin himself, as has been seen, felt that continued hold on office was uncertain. But the only sign of check or friction was a fresh resolution of the assembly in September that the decision with regard to the Clergy Reserves ought not to be withdrawn from the provincial legislature. The project of a grand trunk railway line took definite shape ; railway legislation became the order of the day ; a subsidy was given to start a proper steamship service between Britain and Canada ; the decisive step was taken in introducing a decimal system of currency ; the franchise was reformed and the provincial assembly was increased from a membership of 84 to one of 130. An attempt to reform seigniorial tenures was lost in the Upper Chamber, and that vote lent impetus to the movement which Elgin himself now supported, by which that chamber should definitely become an elective, not a nominated one. Throughout the period, too, the ground for a reasonable reciprocity treaty with the United States was being throughly explored and prepared.

Elgin, then, was able to describe the province, in July, 1853, as " perfectly tranquil and contented,"[1] and to tell his friends that he had applied for leave of absence.

With his departure on leave, and in view of the fact that he returned in 1854 for a brief six months' stay, it might seem that the interest and importance of his work came to a halt at this point. Actually the remaining period, and more especially the last six months, proved perhaps the most remarkable and productive of his whole government. In his absence, and that of his Prime Minister, the political situation inclined to get out of hand. The very cleverness of the new Premier told against him. He never possessed the moral authority of La Fontaine or Baldwin, and he had involved himself in commercial dealings not exactly dishonourable but of doubtful propriety to one in his position. To the earnest radicals it seemed that both he and the Governor-General were much too conservative in their methods and measures ; and

[1] Elgin to Cumming Bruce, 16 July, 1853.

as Brown urged his various policies in Upper
Canada, a cleavage once more threatened between
French and English. As Elgin was determined
to check any such tendency, the more he held the
French in coalition with his ministers, the more
hostile and more numerous grew the radical party
in revolt. Moreover, although McNab and his
Tories had sown their wild oats, and reaped their
futile harvest, even the moderate Conservatives
were disinclined to let Hincks and Morin escape if
they could out-manœuvre and defeat them. When
once a ministry has begun to enter a period of strain,
it is extraordinary how everything seems to conspire
to discredit it. So it happened now. The Imperial Parliament had now (since early in 1853)
left the Clergy Reserves to be dealt with provin-
cially ; but partly because it seemed best to await
the radical change in the constitution of the assembly which would mature in 1854, partly also, I
fancy, because Elgin wished to carry even the
Tories with him when he and his ministry moved,
no legislation on the subject had been proposed in
1853, and the Clear Grit watchdogs had started
barking. Then an odd constitutional accident
tripped up the ministers. Elgin and Hincks did
not return from negotiating the Reciprocity Treaty
at Washington to the province until June, 1854, and
when parliament met on 13 June it had evaded only

135

by a single day a clear breach of the rule that not more than twelve calendar months should intervene between the last sitting in one session, and the first sitting in the next ![1] Further, when, to escape complete defeat on the address, the ministry advised the Governor-General to dissolve the parliament at once, the formal prorogation took place without a single measure having been passed in that session, and the diverse elements in the opposition staged a scene of protest which suggested a comic version of seventeenth-century parliamentary history. There can be no doubt that Lord Elgin was deeply chagrined at this inconclusive ending to a notable assembly. Canadian gossip has it that his face revealed his feelings at the prorogation, and to his wife, who was now in Britain, he wrote : " My parliament has been trying to diminish my sentimentality for this country by behaving very badly, but I have sent them about their business."[2]

From the first, he had counted the defeat of the ministry as probable—" the ultra-Radicals are opposing them " he told his new chief, Sir George Grey ; and the election verified the prophecy.[3] Brown, Mackenzie, and the Reformers of the West entered the fight with immense energy and gusto ;

[1] The Union Act, c. 31.
[2] Letters to Lady Elgin, 24 June, 1854.
[3] Elgin to Sir George Grey, 8 July, 1854.

the Rouge section in Lower Canada had grown in
numbers and ability ; the Tories of all shades were
at least holding their own ; and parliament when
it met was certain to contain three groups, Radical,
Moderate, and Conservative, any one of which by
combining with the second could defeat the third.

It is impossible to doubt that delay over Clergy
Reserve legislation had had much to do with the
split in the West. It is also clear that Elgin himself
had done something to secure that delay. To
judge his conduct impartially, then, it is important
to know why he supported ministers in a policy
which led to defeat.

" If I had allowed the last parliament to deal with the
Clergy Reserves," he wrote to his wife, " no doubt they
would have secularized them ; but they would have
enabled the friends of the endowment to say that the
opinion of the province had not been fairly taken on the
question, and this allegation would certainly have been
very extensively believed in England. In the new parliament the fate of the endowment will be the same, but at
any rate it will be impossible to say that the country was
taken by surprise ; and the division in the Provincial
parliament will probably show that its preservation was
impossible."[1]

It was all the simpler for him to advise a passive
policy, because he knew that if he played his cards
correctly the new assembly would be a moderate

[1] Letters to Lady Elgin, 25 August, 1854.

and not a radical assembly, and that, even if his present ministers should be defeated, a coalition between them and the now chastened Tories could easily and naturally be contrived, and that in such a coalition the ancient and futile phase of Canadian Conservatism would find its complete extinction.

The circumstances of the change of ministers, and of the introduction of a fresh coalition are so important, and the whole affair is so characteristic of Elgin's ideas and methods in politics that they must be given in two hitherto unpublished letters to Sir George Grey :

" Ministers," he wrote on 9 September, " feeling that the House of Assembly had become altogether unmanageable by them, tendered to me yesterday their resignation. Although this plan of retiring before the Speech from the Throne has been answered is a very inconvenient one, and little consistent with British practice, I thought it a less evil to let them retire than oblige them to go on for an indefinite time while the opposition was adjourning the discussion of the speech on all manner of protests, and increasing daily in numbers by the addition of rats from the sinking ship. Besides which, time is of great consequence to me, as I am most desirous to get a strong administration into office before I hand over the government to my successor. Hincks made a statement in the House last night announcing his resignation, which produced, I am told, considerable effect. In office or out he is the most able and powerful man in this country at present. . . . Immediately on my acceptance of Hincks' resignation I sent for Sir Allan McNab. I shall probably know before the mail leaves, whether or not he finds it possible to form an administration. Should he fail, I have other combinations to fall back upon. You need not give yourself any anxiety, for I have no doubt whatever that I shall succeed in making an administration that will be able to conduct the government satisfactorily. The only drawback under which I labour arises from want of time.

"Hincks will not, I believe, come into office on any consideration himself at present, but he will give his support cordially to any administration which will carry out his measures.

"The most important development which has taken place during the general election is the establishment of a regular schism in the ranks of the French Lower Canadians. When I came to this country the great difficulty of governing it arose from the fact that the Lower Canadian French always went together, the consequence of which was that the Upper Canadian party which acted with them always had an overwhelming majority in parliament, and was always accused of governing through a French Roman Catholic influence. I often told the violent British when they were so abusive of my policy that their professed desire to keep down the French was the cause of this cohesion in their ranks, and that, if they would act fairly by the French and allow them to feel that they stood on the same footing as the other Canadian subjects of the Queen, parties analogous to those which existed in Upper Canada would form themselves in Lower Canada. After a few years of ' Justice to Lower Canada ' the result has verified my predictions. We have now a regular Conservative and a regular Radical party in Lower Canada. For the moment it makes a difficulty, but I believe it will turn out to be a great advantage eventually, and tend naturally to the preservation of the Union. French Canadian parties will co-operate with the Upper Canadian with which they have political sympathies, and the division between the provinces be gradually effaced. . . .

" I enclose a copy of a note which I have just received from Mr. Hincks. I have reason to believe that he is doing his utmost to enable Sir Allan McNab to form an administration, and particularly to induce the French Canadians to join him."[1]

The second letter completes the story :

" The arrangements for the new administration progress thus far satisfactorily. I have brought into office the leaders of the Conservative party, thus giving the most emphatic denial to the charge that I had any unconstitutional preference for one party over the other, and those leaders have agreed to take my speech from the Throne as it stands, to carry an address responsive to it, and to bring in measures to give effect to all the recommendations which it contains ; thus furnishing on their part the most conclusive proof that the policy which I had sketched out while acting with the former administration was the only policy suited to the wants and circumstances of the province. I think that this conjuncture besides leading, as I trust it will, to the formation of a stable government, and facilitating the peaceful settlement of some most irritating and harassing questions, will afford a most useful constitutional lesson to my Canadian friends. On the one hand, the inconvenience of taking untenable positions for party purposes, while in opposition, will be felt in many questions ; on the other, the constitutional impartiality of the representative of the

---

[1] Elgin to Sir George Grey, 9 September, 1854.

Crown will be fully vindicated. As you have only lately
become directly concerned with the administration of
Colonial affairs you may not perhaps appreciate all the
importance of this latter demonstration ; but they who
have watched the course of Canadian history during the
last few years, who have noticed the part played in our
local politics by Sir Allan McNab and his followers, and
their systematic endeavour to single out the Governor-
General for attack, and to make him personally responsible for administrative measures which they condemned,
will understand its full moral significance. The extreme
left consisting of a section of the Upper Canadian Liberals
and the new French party, to which I directed your attention in my last letter, are very indignant and exceedingly
annoyed at not having been called into office. They
ascribe their disappointment altogether to the personal
predilections and high Tory sympathies of the Governor-
General, which is rather amusing, considering the reasons
I have for preferring Sir A. McNab, and the reputation
for ultra-liberalism in Colonial matters, which I have
already earned in England. . . . The importance of
this ministerial change arises from the fact that, notwithstanding the theoretical recognition of the constitutional
position of the Governor-General, which has been made
at former periods, every one of my predecessors has been
killed off before he has been able to resume into his councils
men who had gone into violent personal opposition. I
found as you may probably know, a Conservative Government in office when I came here. The reconstruction
by me of a Conservative Government after the stormy
years that have intervened will tend, I think, more than
anything which has yet occurred, to place the Governor-
General in his proper place in the political structure." [1]

[1] Elgin to Sir George Grey, 15 September, 1854.

It was indeed of the first importance to illustrate fully the working of the new system of Colonial parliamentary government, and the relation of the Governor-General to it ; but, in Canadian history, these letters have a further significance. Since the fall of the Tories in 1848, it had become a recognized habit for them, in their attack on the Governor-General and the government, to take to themselves such allies as they could, to advocate any measures, no matter how preposterous, and to attack proposals which all Canadians, including themselves, knew to be essential to Canadian well-being. On British standards such conduct was worse than revolutionary ; it was mere anarchy. Elgin had played a waiting game, and now, by making McNab and his party countersign the Queen's Speech as it stood, and accept literally and entirely all the measures advocated by the late government, he was forcing them to acknowledge their previous factiousness in the most humiliating way. The enemy had not merely surrendered unconditionally ; they had undertaken to serve the victor in obtaining those very objects against which they had previously struggled most bitterly.

There was a further implication—that under existing conditions the best government of Canada was a coalition of the moderates. Elgin's victory was the more resounding, because the terms which he had dictated were not those of a politician maliciously anxious to humble the opposition by extorting excessive concessions, but were most plainly the conditions best fitted to promote Canadian prosperity. If Hincks and his supporters had ceased to be Radicals, when they agreed to co-operate with the Tories, McNab and Macdonald had abandoned for ever the old Tory traditions, and programme. The future lay with Liberal Conservatism.

It was Lord Elgin's ambition to carry through all his more important projects, and then leave his successor a fair field to begin with.[1] Already, on 22 September, both houses had unanimously adopted the Reciprocity Treaty so far as Canada was concerned. Before the end of the year, three of the provinces concerned had done the same, and the Nova Scotian parliament had been called for 2 December on purpose to pass the measure. In October the bill for secularizing the Clergy Reserves was introduced by the Conservative Attorney-General, John A. Macdonald, and carried through all its stages ; and that for abolishing all feudal rights and duties in Lower Canada followed the same course. On 18 December came the adjournment, and when parliament next met, in February, 1855, there would be a new Governor-General.

[1] Elgin to Sir E. Head, 10 October, 1854.

143

It is a vice in biographies much too prevalent, to exaggerate the virtues, powers, and influence of their heroes. Yet, in the present case it is difficult not to make very extensive claims for Lord Elgin. An Edinburgh reviewer,[1] in days before reviews had lost the note of real authority, gave it as his verdict, after the most generous modifications, that " Lord Elgin can hardly be ranked with the first of British statesmen." But, if the Canadian administration be fairly studied, it is hard to see any other position appropriate to his merits. He had perfected the scheme of Colonial parliamentary government now in operation in all our self-governing dominions ; he had tutored a succession of Canadian ministers, and British Colonial Secretaries, in matters of the first importance, and in which their ignorance was of equal magnitude ; he had reconciled the French to the Canadian and Imperial authorities ; and he had indicated the lines of future development in Canadian politics. As will be shown in the next chapter, his economic policy had been equally important and successful. If the impossible could have happened, and Lord Elgin could have, in 1854, transformed himself into a Canadian " citizen," he would have overshadowed all his predecessors or successors in the dominion, and have stood out as the greatest Canadian states-

[1] January, 1873.

144

man of the century. If these facts be fairly weighed, it is not too much to say that only three men at that time in England had either achieved or promised more, or exhibited more genius in parliamentary and administrative life. These were Peel, indubitably ; Gladstone by virtue of his dæmonic, if unbalanced, personality ; and Disraeli, whose entire lack of equipment for serious administration and whose singular absence of the sense of ordinary political realities were covered and atoned for by his glittering genius.

CHAPTER IV

CANADA: ECONOMIC DEVELOP-MENTS TO THE RECIPROCITY TREATY OF 1854

LORD ELGIN'S success in negotiating one of the most useful treaties in the history of Anglo-American relations is usually dealt with as an important but detached appendix to his government of Canada. It will be the object of this chapter to show that it was an essential and necessary part of that government, and, with his concession of full self-government to the Colony, an evidence of his perfect understanding of the needs of the people whom he governed. It is time, indeed, to call a halt to the excessive emphasis laid by the historians of Canada on obvious surface constitutional phenomena; and to exhibit, not the constitutional or the economic history of the province, but the actual life of the community, of which both the political and the economic issues were normal symptoms. A community, some two million strong, had begun to show signs of the complex growth which we call civilization. Its first attempt was naturally to secure complete control of its own political machinery ; but the force behind self-government was the broader, richer, and more complicated existence which the Canadian community had begun to establish for itself by 1846. Out of that new condition came new problems, new leaders and new policies ; and the reign of Elgin in Canada was the watershed period, and he himself the man best fitted to help the new regime to escape from the hampering traditions of the old. Whether for better or worse, the time had come for the organization of material resources, the extension of the provincial life to touch regions outside the province, the clearing out of the way of old difficulties, irritating because really disconnected with the fresh vigour and the spirit of enterprise which now made themselves felt. Before 1837 it had been possible to conceive of a colony which was not self-governing ; after 1850 responsible government was the one constitutional expedient possible for a society that could no longer be treated as, in the old narrow sense, a British possession.

Perhaps the clearest evidence of this new national temper is to be found in the development of railway enterprises throughout the whole of the Elgin period. Between 1850 and 1860 the

mileage increased from 66 to 2,065, and most
of the work of organization took place after
1846.[1] It was part of a great American movement of expansion, and of communications made
necessary by, and then assisting in, that expansion.
First, Canada had competed for the transportation
of inland commodities to the great eastern ports—
Montreal, Boston, New York, Philadelphia. Then
railways joined up lacunæ in the waterways and
finally superseded them. As purely economic
facts, there were the lines linking up Canada with
Boston in 1851, and with Portland in 1852 ; and
the long, confused, but really successful achievement which established a Grand Trunk line from
East of Quebec to the West of the Upper province.
As strategical and political facts there stood the
greater confusion and much less perfect success
of the line which was to link up the Maritime
Provinces with Canada proper. Interest in railways, while not always a proof of political virtue,
was the distinguishing mark between the old school
of Canadian politicians and the new. Baldwin
and La Fontaine belonged to the earlier world, and
were really gently but inevitably thrust out of
political prominence by actors and movements
which they neither understood, nor cared for.
The leaders into the immediate future were men

[1] Skelton, *Life of Sir A. T. Galt*, p. 75.

like John A. Macdonald, Alexander Galt, and among the French, Cartier ; financiers, business men, opportunists, shifty or steady, men who saw that Canada unlike older countries could not afford to be absorbed in merely political concerns. It was quaint evidence that a new world had arisen, when Sir Allan McNab, petty jobber as he was in politics, but yet with a wonderfully sharp scent for anything that spelt private advantage, declared in 1854 that " his platform was Railways." It was natural that neither Elgin nor his partner in Liberal imperial policy, Grey, should take much part in railway affairs. These lay outside their natural sphere of operations—indeed the extension of self-government was largely caused by the development of important regions of Canadian life over which neither Governor nor Colonial Secretary cared to exert any supervision. It was, of course, Grey's concern to consider the making of an intercolonial railway, linking up the scattered colonies ; and he cannot be blamed for the halts and changes in carrying out that project. Caution, not unjustified, and a spirit of economy at home ; the loud talk of independence or annexation to the United States indulged in by the very business men who were managing railway exploitation— these things checked the ardent temper of the Colonial Secretary. " Anxious as I am to bring forward the railway scheme," he wrote to Elgin in 1849, " and firmly as I am still convinced that it would prove to be a measure of the greatest political advantage, I am compelled to acknowledge that in the present state of public opinion it is a proposal which could not prudently be made."[1] A little later he dwelt on the harm done to possible investment of British capital in Canada by the Rebellion Losses Act, and the irresponsible chatter of the annexationists.

One cannot say that Lord Elgin's private letters betray more than an ordinary interest in the subject ; but he backed Hincks up in his many railway measures—as for example his Guarantees Act of 1849, which lent State support to deserving enterprises, and the municipal acts which made it only too easy for districts to overstrain their credit in the support of railway construction. It was partly because he appreciated the need for men like Hincks that he spoke so warmly of their ability, although not necessarily of their characters. Where railway enterprise linked up, as it so often did, the province with the American Republic, he was at his very best as the representative of the empire. He had a happy faculty for understanding that Colony and Republic must in the future be even more and more closely bound up together com-

[1] Grey to Elgin, 25 January, 1849.

THE EARL OF ELGIN.
Reproduced from a Daguerreotype taken at Montreal in 1849

mercially, and socially, without fearing any unfortunate consequences. Partly because he was a natural optimist, partly because he believed in the power of the British tradition, and the superior excellence of British methods in government, he " accepted the universe "—which meant fraternizing freely with his American neighbours. He never sent Grey a more characteristic letter than when he described his visit to Boston to celebrate a great railway occasion there :

" My little holiday, as you style it, has not been spent altogether in idleness, as I have lately travelled in 8 days nearly 1,500 miles, and met, firstly all the United States, President included, at Boston, and secondly my Montreal friends. I hope that I have broken, or, as I should rather say, thawed a little the ice in the latter place, and as to the former, it is Crampton's opinion, I believe, that I did no harm by my visit there. Nothing certainly could be more cordial than the conduct of the Bostonians throughout, and there was a scrupulous avoidance of any topic that could wound British or Canadian susceptibilities. The only exception was Webster, who made a speech in very bad taste on the occasion of the President's reception. I took care, however, not to arrive till the day following, so I escaped all this. We had a dinner on the Boston Common for 3,500 persons, at which some good speeches were made, Everett's especially so." [1]

Without depreciating the Governor-General's part in the development of Canadian railways, it

[1] Elgin to Grey, 26 September, 1851.

was related to that of his advisers as the rôle of any distinguished director is to that of heads of executive departments.

But railways were only one mode in which the new expansion exhibited itself. The real centre of interest lay in the general growth in production, and wealth, and enterprise throughout the provinces, and in the new relations with the outside world which that growth created. In days not so very far in the past, Canadian colonists had led first a struggling, and then a self-sufficing life—having no margin of production to send outside the district, and with wealth sufficient only to make trifling purchases in external markets of what might be called necessary luxuries. What there was in the way of timber or wheat, Great Britain allowed to enter with a substantial preference over all rivals ; or, if the district concerned lay on the great lakes, the cheapness of water transportation made up in part for the heavy custom duties of the United States. Economically, Canada had no history, for she had no economics more complex than the task of keeping the wolf, actual and symbolical, from the door.

Two circumstances changed this unambitious and peaceful era. In the first place not merely did the population increase enormously in numbers, but the activity of the individual colonist, the power and knowledge of the rising communities, and, with all backsets, the real wealth of the whole province, French and British, suffered a revolutionary development. By 1853—to select the year in which Lord Elgin circulated a much read despatch on Canadian conditions—the imports into Canada for the year were worth £4,168,457 8s. 5d., and the exports £2,888,214; more than 1,300 ships entered at the two St. Lawrence ports, and more than a million tons of traffic were carried on the Chambly, St. Lawrence, and Welland canals.[1] One meets everywhere with groans and complaints of poverty, but they were growing pains which caused the outcry. Jeshurun was beginning to grow fat and to kick. With margins of Canadian products ready for export, with actual profits free to be spent on imported goods ; and with continually increasing convenience in despatch and transportation, Canada had ceased to be self-contained. She had acquired the first essential for starting a diplomatic career —she had new needs, and she had commodities suitable for exchange.

In the second place the free trade budgets of Sir Robert Peel, but more especially the great change in 1846, affected a colony like Canada even more than it did Great Britain. When the British Act of 1843 had made milling a new source of profit

---

[1] Elgin to Newcastle, 5 September, 1853.

to Canadians, the colonists had grown confident that, in exchange for the possible disadvantages of the British connection, they had a guarded market in Britain for some of their chief natural products, and this was the more consoling because even in their less protectionist moods the inhabitants of the United States still exacted heavy customs duties. With 1846 the British Empire on its old basis of trade preference for colonies ceased to exist ; and to complicate the system the navigation laws which logically should have gone overboard with protection still remained to hamper colonial traffic, and increase the cost of shipping out of Canadian harbours. The truth is that imperial considerations proper are always a second thought on the part of British legislators, and Free Traders in 1846 carried out a great British measure without any considerable thought for the communities whose existence they had up to 1846 shaped by trade regulations planned at least as much in the interests of the mother country as for the colonies. " I care not whether you be a Protectionist or a Free Trader," Elgin complained to Grey in 1848, when things looked very black in Canada, " it is the inconsistency of imperial legislation, and not the adoption of one policy rather than another which is the bane of the Colonies."[1]

[1] Elgin to Grey, 16 November, 1848.

To make a long story short, the prolonged fight in Canada for some kind of commercial reciprocity with the United States, was the consequence of this development of Canadian power of production and marketable margins ; and of the sudden jar given to the whole pre-existing economic fabric by the catastrophic introduction of free trade in Britain.

As a shrewd and unbiased witness from outside, Lord Elgin seized at once on the commercial grievances and difficulties of the colonists, and the obvious way out. From the very first, for he alluded to reciprocity in a letter to Grey before he had been three months in Canada,[1] he felt the seriousness of the situation, and saw how obviously the United States provided one solution or another of the problem.

By May, 1848, he had left the Colonial Secretary in no doubt as to his views.

" The true policy in this matter according to my judgment is to secure for H.M.'s subjects in Canada free access to the markets of the States, and all the advantages with respect to reduction of freights which competition in the St. Lawrence and the Ocean will afford. This system will undoubtedly lead to much intercourse between the neighbouring countries, and to the multiplication of their commercial relations, but you cannot prevent this even if you desired to do so. So long as you

---

[1] Elgin to Grey, 26 March, 1847.

adhered to the policy of protection you raised an artificial
barrier between them. You enabled the Canadian to
point to the preferences which he enjoyed in the mother
country as the price paid for the drawback, real or supposed, of the connection. Now, the least you can do
for him, after depriving him of these preferences, is to
put him on as good a footing as his neighbour : to enable
him to say when tempted, ' What should I gain by re-
nouncing my allegiance ? ' "[1]

On the other hand, and more especially when
the business men of Montreal had surrendered to
annexationist views, he acknowledged that if nothing were done it would be quite hopeless to attempt
to maintain the connection with Great Britain.

" A large portion of the produce of Canada now pays
duty to the government of the States and is sold across
the lines. Prices are kept down at a lower level on this
side the frontier. If the impediment which prevents
their rising to an equality be not removed by negotiation
it will be by annexation."

But negotiation with the American government
was no easy task.

To begin with, the United States, much more
than Britain, had carried into international bargaining the cool and merciless methods of business.
Even in so restrained a document as that which
conveyed to Elgin in 1854 the instructions of the
Foreign Office, the writer, speaking no doubt

[1] 23 May, 1848.

from deep experience, bade Elgin note " as a principle never to be lost sight of in negotiating with the United States, that no concession can safely be made to that government except in return for corresponding concession on its part."[1] The keenness of American bargaining was sharpened by the national habit of regarding everything desired by Americans as a natural right, and everything expected by the other side as an attempt to defraud the Union. Nothing that Machiavelli ever taught has proved half so helpful in the establishing of a great power, as the American capacity for turning rank greed into something savouring of righteousness.

Further, in view of this coming bout of huxtering, the Canadians did not seem to have much to offer save their earnest desire for greater markets. They could promise open doors, but the United States, safe in its home markets and " unexampled prosperity " did not keenly desire these ; and even those who stood to gain in general forgot such petty advantages in the pleasure of excluding the provincials, as they called them, from greater. There were the St. Lawrence, and the canals from Welland to Montreal, and there were those across the border, to whom such access would be a gain. But, after all, the St. Lawrence route was a competitor

[1] Instructions to Lord Elgin, F.O., 4 May, 1854.

for sea-borne traffic with American routes, especially in the State of New York. As a matter of fact, it was not until the peril of severe restriction in fishing in the waters of the British Maritime provinces became imminent that reciprocity was taken seriously by the American government and nation ; and so long as Canada alone of the British provinces attempted to bargain, the fisheries did not enter.

The nature of the American constitution, too, presented peculiar difficulties, where the subject of negotiations was commercial, and affected a variety of scattered interests. Here Elgin may speak for himself, for no one has better analysed the subtle difficulty involved. It was in 1850, and Sir Henry Bulwer had spent some part of his four days' visit to Toronto in recording his impressions of American institutions. Elgin's reflections on what he heard were shrewd :

" The fact is that the Yankee system is our old Colonial system with, in certain cases, the principle of popular election substituted for that of nomination by the Crown. Mr. Fillmore stands to his Congress very much in the same relation in which I stood to my assembly in Jamaica, though with the utmost deference I venture to think I managed my refractory crew better than he does his. There is the same absence of effective responsibility in the conduct of legislation, the same want of concurrent action between the parts of the political machine. The whole business of legislation in the American Congress, as well as in the State legislatures is conducted in the same manner in which railway business was conducted in the House of Commons, at a time when it is to be feared that, notwithstanding the high standard of honour in the British Parliament, there was a good deal of jobbing. For instance, our reciprocity measure was pressed by us at Washington last session just as a railway bill in 1845 or 1846 would have been pressed in parliament. There was no government to deal with. The interests of the Union as a whole, and distinct from local and sectional interests, had no organ in the representative bodies—it was all a question of canvassing this member of Congress or the other. It is easy to perceive that under such a system jobbing must become not the exception but the rule."[1]

Obviously it was perilous work for agents of a foreign power to conduct lobbying and jobbing on their own account ; yet so accurate is Elgin's description of the process that, even in 1854, and with the Reciprocity treaty actually signed, it took some measure of undue pressure on individuals to get the sanction of the Senate.

But even should the measure find some sort of hearing, it was practically certain to be caught into some one or other of the great political whirlpools and finally wrecked through no fault of its own. The early fifties saw the slavery question predominant everywhere, and down to 1854 Nebraska-Kansas affairs arrayed parties in fierce antagonism

[1] Elgin to Grey, 1 November, 1850.

to one another. There was always the chance that some indirect connection with the slave question might break the back of the bill. Even in June, 1854, when the treaty was signed, and although the South was for the time being happy and victorious, Crampton reported from Washington a rumour that " the South are going to move as an amendment (to the treaty) that the Fugitive Slave Law should be extended to Canada ! "[1] But annexationist intrigue was the most serious of the whirlpools to be feared. Nothing does less credit to the honour of American diplomacy in the middle nineteenth century than the steady current in favour of annexing Canada, directly or indirectly, which queered the course for honest diplomatists on both sides. So inveterate was the habit that although Elgin acknowledged Marcy, the Secretary of State in 1854, to be a frank and honest dealer, the documents and instructions issued by that statesman just before the final negotiations contain unfortunate phrases about stimulating and extending in Canada " an increased regard and interest for this country and its institutions " and the wish of the government " to tighten the bonds which unite the two countries."[2] It it just possible that the Southern politicians were

[1] Crampton to Elgin, 25 June, 1854.
[2] Tansill, *The Canadian Reciprocity Treaty of 1854*, pp. 61–62.

CANADA: ECONOMIC DEVELOPMENTS

ultimately led to support the measure by a grotesque perversion of this annexationist argument. They feared, it seems, lest reciprocity, bringing annexation in its train, would add to the strength of their Northern rivals ; but, since Elgin had convinced all and sundry that reciprocity was the antidote to annexation, those who at first came to curse the measure stayed to bless it.

Apart from the uncertainty as to the advantages which Canada had to offer in exchange, the chief difficulty on the Canadian side came from the dislocated and competitive attempts of all the provinces to get something along with Canada, and the tendency in such competition for the provincial agents to present themselves with foolish eagerness *in forma pauperis*. Whatever Bulwer's faults were as British representative at Washington in 1850, he was a quick and judicious observer, and one may watch his restlessness and irritation, as the combined lack of unity and dignity on the part of the British North American colonies undermined his efforts.

" I have been very ready to hope," he wrote in July, 1850, to Elgin, " that all the agitation which has taken place respecting our bill would not injure it, and that New Brunswick and Nova Scotia might eventually be admitted into it. But I must confess that the first views which I formed on this subject seem the most correct. The measure has certainly lost ground owing to the stir made about it. The conviction that we must have it, or that the colonies will separate from us, and that if it is so much desired by the Colonies it must be very prejudicial to the U.S. has gained upon public opinion here."[1]

It has been far too little noticed how great a service Elgin rendered to all the provinces by forcing them to accept him as their representative, and by putting an end to the competing offers and claims through which they revealed their own weakness, and stimulated the cupidity of their antagonists. It was Elgin who first taught British North America the value of confederation in diplomacy ; and certainly the dominion has never been better served than in the days when Elgin imposed an unnatural unity upon the colonies, and made his bargain with Marcy in the name of all.

In the long and confused negotiations between the two governments which extended from 1846 down to June, 1854, three quite distinct periods may be noticed—the period of concurrent legislation, down to 1852, although, so long as the Fillmore administration lasted, efforts still continued to be made at legislation in Congress ; a doubtful period from September, 1852, in which Crampton made two distinct efforts to arrange a project of agreement with the Fillmore, and then with the

[1] Bulwer to Elgin, 11 July, 1850.

Pierce governments, both proving failures ; and the short decisive action of Lord Elgin who received authority from the Foreign Office on 4 May, 1854, to attempt a forlorn hope, signed his treaty with W. L. Marcy on 5 June, and had it fully accepted by the United States, Senate, Congress, and President on 5 August.

It is not easy to follow all the steps taken by either party to the bargain in the earliest period. In a sense it may be regarded as beginning when, on 10 March, 1845, Lord Aberdeen, the Foreign Minister in Peel's administration, communicated to the American Ambassador in London, Everett, the concession of privileges to American fisheries in the Bay of Fundy.

" In thus communicating to Mr. Everett the liberal intentions of H.M. Government," continued Aberdeen, " the undersigned desires to call Mr. Everett's attention to the fact that the produce of the labour of the British Colonial fishermen is at the present moment excluded by prohibitory duties on the part of the United States from the markets of that country ; and the undersigned would submit to Mr. Everett that the moment at which the British Government are making a liberal concession to U.S. trade might well be deemed favourable for a counter-concession on the part of the United States to British trade by the reduction of the duties which operate so prejudicially to the interests of British Colonial fishermen."[1]

---

[1] H.M. Secretary of State for Foreign affairs to the Envoy and Minister Plenipotentiary of the U.S.A., 10 March, 1845.

Needless to say, nothing was done. It might have been possible, and Canadians like W. H. Merritt thought it folly not to make the effort, to secure better terms for Canada when Great Britain opened her doors to foreign importation, especially of grain, in 1846. But if not Peel, then the convinced Free Traders who took over from him, and of whom Earl Grey was the most resolute and doctrinaire, refused to compromise their principles by any kind of trading bargains, or any suggestion of retaliation for the sake of Canada. Until the United States began to feel the pressure of fishery restrictions, that was the last moment at which Britain and her North American colonies had a good chance of striking a bargain. Driven by the commercial misfortunes which followed in Canada on the establishment of free trade in Britain, the Canadian Government, and later those of New Brunswick and Nova Scotia, attempted to secure something from their neighbours.[1] In May, 1846, at the instigation especially of Merritt, an address to the Crown was carried to urge diplomatic action at Washington ; but although a favourable answer was returned from London, and although Aberdeen communicated at once with his minister at Washington, the United States had too much on hand,

[1] It may be remembered that, from 1846, Canadian goods could be sent in bond for shipment through the U.S.

especially in Mexico, to trouble about Canadian trade. In the meantime the Canadian Government first equated the duties on British and American goods in July, 1847, and then, as the bargaining grew in volume, in 1849 they offered, in a bill, complete reciprocity in all products of farm, mine and forest. It was indeed clear that " Barkis was willin'." A constant correspondence was maintained in these years between the Governor-General and the British agents at Washington —first Crampton, then Bulwer, and then once more Crampton. A stream of Canadian agents moved between Montreal and Toronto and Washington, Tiffany, Merritt, Wilson, Hincks and others ; and Lord Elgin kept a steady pressure on the home Government through Grey, the constantly recurring text of his discourse being " Reciprocity or Annexation." In the course of these weary years down to 1852 it was not surprising that American methods should occasionally seem rather unlovely to one accustomed to directer means of action. This kind of irritation appears most conspicuously in Elgin's correspondence in 1850 and 1851. He reported to Grey the case of an employee of the United States Government who warned Bulwer that no measure was ever carried through against which there was anything like opposition, without the aid of a liberal expenditure and a steady press propaganda.[1] About the same time a certain Mr. I. D. Andrews turned up—of whom more later—not altogether to Elgin's satisfaction.

" I have had a nice specimen of the model republic and underpaid officials in a certain Yankee Consul to Canada who has been here last week," he wrote to Grey on 22 November, 1850. " He is employed by his own Government to write a report on the trade between Canada and the United States, in order to aid Congress in coming to a decision on the Reciprocity question. He gives me to understand that he has very sound views on this subject, and that if he had command of a considerable sum of money, others might be induced to take the same."

In the following year he reported " a letter from Crampton, disclosing in strict confidence an amount of villany at Washington beyond what either he or I were prepared for. The upshot is that the whole question of our getting or not getting Reciprocity appears to hinge on our booking up £20,000."[2] It is useless to raise hands in self-righteous horror ; but where the machinery of government by which a commercial pact is secured is of the character so shrewdly analysed by Lord Elgin, some kind or other of dingy corruption is the inevitable product.

[1] Elgin to Grey, 11 December, 1850.
[2] Elgin to Grey, 15 November, 1851.

Meanwhile in House and Senate there had been much cry and little wool. In 1848, 1849, 1850, 1851, 1852, and even into 1853, a series of bills were introduced in Washington with no effect whatever. It had almost become a habit for the President to allude to the subject in December, and for Congress to devise some fresh but inconspicuous way of shelving the efforts of the session. The administration at Washington had voted for legislation rather than treaty, and the ghosts of dead and mutilated bills ought by 1852 to have haunted the White House and the residence of the Secretary of State. The British minister at Washington, J. F. Crampton, had lost confidence in what he called in 1852 " this rather hopeless business."

" We have very little discretion in the matter as things now stand," he wrote ; " for it is neither the British Government nor the United States administration which can bring in the measure, but the representatives of some of the American interests concerned in it. If we hurl the means of acting upon these interests by an effective retaliation, such as putting on a discriminating duty to their wheat in England, it would be another question ; but this seems not probable ; and indeed the proposal which was made to me some time ago, of which I wrote to you, serves to show that they feel that it is a matter in which they can act pretty much as suits their convenience, either to do or not to do, without much risk of damage either at home or abroad."[1]

---

[1] Crampton to Elgin, 15 April, 1852.

The fact was that for working purposes Canada counted merely as one of the many "interests" which were importuning Congress to secure a private advantage ; and neither Canada nor her sister provinces could convince the other interests through which legislation became possible, that it was worth while listening. The use of the St. Lawrence and the canals was brought forward, withdrawn, and then reintroduced as a make-weight in the argument. After 1850 plain sugges-tions of retaliation were made, and Elgin more than half consented to them, but it was clear that most of the retaliating projects would accomplish nothing beyond irritating American opinion.

The really decisive factor in the situation came in the Eastern fisheries ; and from the end of 1849 the idea of some settlement of that question, dovetailed into a reciprocity agreement, entered the field, and remained really dominant to the end.[1] The same factor, in spite of the American inclination for legislation, pretty decisively forced the whole argument into the usual diplomatic channels.

The middle period, corresponding roughly to the years 1852 and 1853, formed a kind of inter-regnum in which action by convention took the

[1] See instructions to Sir H. L. Bulwer on taking over his embassy.

place of legislative action, but with equally futile results.

In September, 1852, Crampton was engaged in negotiating some kind of treaty with Fillmore's expiring administration, not perfectly happy, as he reported to Lord Elgin, about the threats of retaliation in which Canada was indulging. In December Elgin reported to Pakington that Hincks had just received confidentially from Mr. Crampton the draft of a convention with the United States. "We have not had much time to consider it, but I think I can undertake to say that if carried out as proposed it will give much satisfaction here."[1] The terms proposed by Crampton included reciprocity in all natural products, the throwing open of the sea fisheries of the colonies to the United States, the free admission of fish, cured and fresh, into the United States, the opening of the navigation of the St. Lawrence and the Canals, and the inclusion of coal among the articles to be admitted free. Not even the pacific and free-trading spirit of my Lords of the Board of Trade could avoid the conclusion, drawn from the American statement of the case, "that the proposals of the United States in the shape in which they now present themselves to H.M. Government are such as my Lords cannot entertain on any grounds of advan-

[1] Elgin to Pakington, 24 December, 1852.

tage to the commercial interests of the British Empire." [1] So another pale ghost was added to those already encompassing the argument for reciprocal trade.

The last effort, before Elgin came to settle things by a kind of magic, was made after Franklin Pierce and W. L. Marcy established themselves in office in March, 1853. The situation looked more hopeful. The Democrats and the South were in power, free-trade sentiment was increasing ; and there was more than a probability of a great victory over anti-slavery agitation in the Kansas-Nebraska affair. The likelihood that reciprocity with Canada would stave off annexation, and so prevent the North from counting Canada among the non-slavery States of the Union, was also said to be influencing the party in power, who preferred annexations, if such were to be made, in the South. The fishery business, too, was exerting more than a gentle pressure on the legislators. In 1852 both Britain and the provinces had taken steps to strengthen the control of fisheries in Eastern waters, and while the greatest caution and consideration were displayed by the Imperial Government, the American Government realized for the first time that Britain and her Colonies had something worth paying for

[1] F.O. correspondence with the Board of Trade, Report, 20 April, 1853.

in their hands. There was the usual bluster in Congress, Daniel Webster setting the tone in a bullying public oration. A Massachusetts senator, in familiar fashion, told all and sundry "that if Great Britain wants a war undoubtedly she can have it," and another from Texas, applying the method of the gun and the bowie knife in international affairs, even prepared to find cannon "the last available argument that could be used."[1]

Meanwhile Marcy and Crampton, calling in the redoubtable I. D. Andrews to assist them, prepared a fresh *projet* in August and September. The concrete difficulties which presented themselves were the inclusion of coal among free articles ; permission for the registry of British-built ships when they became the property of American citizens, and the question of American bounties to fishermen. It must be added that the tone of quiet assumption on the part of the American Government that what their subjects desired, although contrary to existing treaty rights, should out of hand be delivered up, must have proved extremely irritating to the diplomatists of the other side. "The convention of 1818," wrote Marcy in an authoritative despatch to Buchanan in London, "excludes the citizens of the United States from the inshore fisheries—that is from taking fish from within a

[1] Tansill, *op. cit.* pp. 42–45.

marine league of the British shores ; *but it cannot be expected that they will in all instances respect this boundary.*"[1]

Once more the British Board of Trade intervened heavily, criticizing the American counter-proposal as " such a one as they cannot advise H.M. Government to entertain. They confine their counter-proposal to the free exchange of a limited number of articles of raw produce with our British American Colonies, claiming in return the admission of American vessels to the navigation of our North American rivers, and to the right of fishing without restriction on our coasts."

" It will be for the Earl of Clarendon," they concluded, " to decide whether the considerations of general policy affecting the question are of a kind to render it expedient with a view to the settlement of the points at issue between the United States and this country to admit conditions which in a commercial point of view my Lords must regard as inequitable."[2]

Clarendon's view, expressed in a note to Crampton at Washington, was that " in our present divergence of views it may be better to suspend for a while the pending negotiations until we can see our way more clearly towards an approximation of those views."[3]

[1] Tansill, *op. cit.* pp. 56–66.
[2] B. of T. report to the F.O., 18 November, 1853.
[3] Clarendon to Crampton, 2 February, 1854.

So all earlier *projets*, bills, and missions had failed. The way was now clear for the final effort ; but it cannot be too clearly stated that the situation seemed as dark as possible, and when the British Government authorized Lord Elgin, in 1854, to pass through Washington on his way to Quebec, they had few bright hopes. " It is scarcely indeed to be supposed," read his instructions, " that under the most favourable circumstances you could finally conclude an arrangement at Washington within the limited time to which, in the first instance, your stay there must necessarily be restricted."[1]

Lord Elgin had indeed many qualifications for the coming encounter with Mr. Marcy and the American Government. He had to a unique degree the patience, tact, and understanding of an opponent's motives which the occasion called for. He had served an apprenticeship of nearly seven years in governing a people almost as democratic as the Americans of the States. On several occasions already he had proved himself acceptable to his Southern neighbours, able not merely to orate in set terms but to make himself socially agreeable. He knew the ins and outs of the case for reciprocity, and his intimate connection with Hincks was now peculiarly useful to him. In addition to all this he carried with him to Washington the

[1] F.O. instructions to the Earl of Elgin, 4 May, 1854.

status of a great and successful proconsul, and the additional glory, in a democratic country, of his title. It was not his business to draw up *de novo* articles for agreement ; for the negotiations and bills of the last seven years had this at least of positive merit that they had defined the issues : liberty for the American fishermen to fish freely on the North-Eastern coasts, with reciprocal rights for provincial fishermen on the Eastern United States coasts : the possible inclusion of the British Pacific coast and the coast of Florida in the arrangement ; the list of articles for which reciprocal freedom of trade was to be granted, coal especially raising a vexed question : the use of canals, British and American : the relation of Newfoundland to the general project ; and the period through which the agreement should be defined as lasting. Thanks to Laurence Oliphant's jaunty style on the one side, and to a natural reaction towards depreciation on the other, there has been too much looseness of phrase in defining Elgin's share in the arrangement. As has been said above, the issues had been defined through seven years of failure, but neither the purely Canadian statesmen, nor their sympathetic friends across the border, had done more than this. Diplomatic success consists partly in definition, but far more largely in carrying out the project desired, and in May, 1854, every one who had hitherto attempted to make a convention or secure the passing of an American Reciprocity Bill had had to confess utter failure. It was Elgin's chief glory that he took all that had been done before, and brought it to completion. It was due to him too that the Treaty of 1854 was a wonderfully favourable settlement for Canada, including in its schedule of articles such unexpected items as coal, and while conceding the North-Eastern fishery privileges, excluding dangerous claims on the Pacific. The peculiar position of Newfoundland had threatened trouble, and an undue share of the plenipotentiary's instructions had dealt, not very successfully, with suitable formulæ to save the situation ; but Elgin found the happy term that ended the difficulty—" the provisions and stipulations of the foregoing Articles shall extend to the Island of Newfoundland *so far as they are applicable to that Colony* "[1]—words whose judicious indefiniteness enabled the Treaty to be ratified and Newfoundland to come in late without disturbance of any vested interests, French or otherwise.

But his chief glory lay in the amazing speed and certainty with which the whole affair was settled. The real trouble in the past had been that the process was long drawn out ; interest flagged ; opposing interests had time to develop their

[1] Reciprocity Treaty, article VI.

campaign ; the colonists were induced to specify their conflicting claims and cases ; and Congress, always ready to delay and criticize, was bound to reject the final product. But Elgin came, saw, and conquered. He arrived in Washington on 26 May ; he signed the Treaty on 5 June, and as he carefully specifies, he left on the first train from Washington after that event. His rapid progress was the more astonishing because he had not only to settle terms with the Secretary of State ; but to feel his way, especially among Democratic senators, towards a probable majority. Always allowing for Oliphant's cheerful fancy and jaunty style, there was something in his jest that during the critical ten days all his and Elgin's most intimate friends were Democrats ; and he was recording perhaps Elgin's greatest achievement when he wrote :

" At last, after we had been receiving the hospitalities at Washington for about ten days, Lord Elgin announced to Mr. Marcy that, if the Government were prepared to adhere to their promise to conclude a treaty of Recipro-city with Canada, he could assure the President that he would find a majority of the Senate in its favour, including several prominent Democrats."

His calculations were correct, for whatever trouble there was in bringing the Treaty safely through the Senate stage it passed that body by a swingeing majority of 32 to 11. Diplomatic and

military history are alike in this, that on the way
to pass a final judgment on great campaigns one
has first to lose a sense of the chief directing mind
in the work of the subordinates : but in both the
sound critic can always be sure of the commander
who won the battle. As Napoleon won at Auster-
litz, or if you please, Marengo, so Elgin and no
other must get credit for snatching his treaty from
the hands of the fates who had wrecked all earlier
attempts ; for doing this in an astonishingly brief
negotiation ; and for securing terms as satisfactory
as they were unexpected.

There was one humble and inconspicuous hero
of the day, who claimed the chief credit for himself
in this great matter, and whose claims have been
more or less acknowledged by recent American and
Canadian historians,[1] Mr. Israel D. Andrews,
American citizen, United States Consul at St.
John's, and ultimately, for his sins or merits, Consul-
General for the Republic in Canada. Mr. Andrews
flits across the pages of the correspondence of that
time with something of the omnipresence of the
mosquito and the assiduity of the competent
bagman. His place would have been more accur-
ately settled had his advocates consulted more
largely their sense of humour. He did much, both

[1] See especially Skelton, *Life of Sir A. T. Galt*, pp. 288 seq.,
and Tansill, *op. cit.*

in the United States and in the Canadian provinces, to keep the issue of Reciprocity to the fore—Mr. Lloyd George would have found him an ideal election organizer. His report on the question was exhaustive and admirable. He kept constantly in touch not only with Washington, but also with Toronto, Montreal, New Brunswick and Nova Scotia. He was consulted by Mr. Marcy in all that statesman did for Reciprocity in 1853 ; and in 1854, as will be seen below, he had so far arrogated to himself the headship over the British provincials that he was engaged in organizing a conference of the provinces when Elgin came to Washington. Perhaps his most notable achievement, however, was that he successfully solicited money from three Governments, all of which, except perhaps the British Imperial Government, seem to have taken him at his own valuation. What he gained from the British side may be inferred from the letter which follows from Lord Elgin to Lord Clarendon, the Foreign Secretary in Aberdeen's cabinet. It was left to an admirable American historian to reveal the fact that during the very months when he was using Canadian money to further Canadian ends, he was also drawing on the funds of the Republic for the corruption or education of the Maritime Provinces—$840 to one gentleman in New Brunswick " for certain purposes of a government and legislative character," $3,900 "for Election Expenses for Government candidate, etc." and other sums " paid privately and by myself to officials, leading persons, and the press, and to others from whom it was not proper to ask for or to expect vouchers ; " in all two lump sums paid over by Marcy, amounting to at least $22,000 dollars.[1]

He pestered Elgin with ill-written letters dashed off in haste as a self-elected lobbier for the act between the signing and the completion of the Treaty ; and could one but lose the sense of his crude absurdity and foolish persistency, it might be possible to think that the chief honours were his. Nothing in all his life for Reciprocity so became him as, according to his own account, the happy ending of the struggle. The description is taken from the long memorandum of services presented later to Lord Elgin ; the occasion was the last four and twenty hours in which the House could pass the bill which the terms of the treaty made necessary :

" Early on Thursday morning I saw Mr. Baily [2] again, and met him by appointment at the committee room at 12. We remained closeted together till 2 p.m. I presented to him the features of the bill, the arguments in its favour, and urged the necessity of immediate action in the House. . . . His final decision was that he would not attempt to pass the bill through the House at that

[1] Tansill, *op. cit.* pp. 67–73. [2] Mr. Baily had charge of the Bill.

session. Mr. Baily went to his lodgings exhausted and determined to do nothing. The bill was left at 4 p.m. this day locked up in his desk at the Capitol ; Congress would adjourn in twenty hours. I remained on the ground all night, confident that by vigorous action there was a chance for the bill. I entered into new obligations for the payment of money to the extent of several thousands. At 4 o'clock, Friday morning, an attempt was made, Mr. Baily not present, to bring up the bill, which failed by about 40 majority against it. It was then generally conceded that it could not pass.

" I made further arrangements, sent for Attorney-General Cushing, and induced him personally to persuade members to act ; and bargained with two Virginians for eight hundred dollars each, provided the bill should pass, to bring in Mr. Baily ' dead or alive.' He had refused others. This was six in the morning. Congress adjourned until 9. At 9.30 Mr. Baily came, our forces were arranged ; at a preconcerted moment Mr. Baily moved the bill, and, although strenuously opposed by the chairman, Committee of Commerce, and others, passed it. This great measure sought for so many years was at last consummated."[1]

This may or may not be true history, but it is excellent journalism, and at worst outdoes Defoe.

It may be unfair to cite the man who won the laurels to give evidence against a defeated candidate, who still held that the victory was his ; but there is a letter of Elgin's to Clarendon so characteristic

[1] Memorandum among Lord Elgin's papers in Andrews' handwriting, undated and unsigned, but seemingly presented to Elgin as he returned to England from Canada.

of its author, so full of little touches about the great negotiation, and so obviously correct in its estimate of this incomplete adventurer, that it must be given almost entire. The occasion of it was that Andrews was seeking to balance his accounts, and approached a Nova Scotian minister, through whom the news came to the British cabinet, Molesworth and Clarendon in particular ; and this is Elgin's private statement to the latter—the letter was written in August, 1855.

" If Sir W. Molesworth desires accurate information respecting Mr. Andrews, I recommend him to seek it, not from Nova Scotia, but from either Mr. Hincks or Mr. Ross of Canada, both of whom are now in this country. All my communications with Mr. Andrews, excepting perhaps one or two formal notes of acknowledgment written during the earlier period of our acquaintance,[1] passed through one or other of these gentlemen. Mr. A. was always very anxious to establish a direct corres-pondence with me ; but although I desired to show all courtesy to a functionary of the Government of the United States, I soon perceived that his object was to obtain from me something which he could construe into an authority to incur indefinite expenditure in some manner not very explainable, for the promotion, as he alleged, of the interests of Reciprocity of trade between the North American provinces with (sic) the U.S. Even if I had had the will, I had not the power to pledge the Imperial Govern-ment to any secret expenditure, and I therefore thought it

---

[1] I have found the draft of only one of these, written appar-ently in November, 1850.

necessary to make all my communications to him through the Provincial ministers, who could deal only with Provincial funds, and who would not sanction any expenditure of such funds which they were not prepared to justify in the local parliament. This course has no doubt given umbrage to Mr. A., but I think the result has shown that it proceeded from no excess of caution. Having said so much I shall now give you in as few words as I can the history of our official connection with this gentleman.

" Mr. Andrews presented himself at Montreal in 1848, or 1849, I forget which, in the capacity of U.S. Consul at Fredericton. He professed to be a warm friend to reciprocity of trade between the provinces and the U.S. ; and to be commissioned by his Government to draw up a report on the subject of the commercial intercourse between the countries. I cannot say that I conceived any very high opinion of Mr. A., but it was obvious that the fate of reciprocity in Congress might be more or less affected by the colour of his report. Sir H. Bulwer was of the same opinion, for I found that when he visited me in the winter of 1880 he had already to a certain extent aided Mr. A. Shortly before this period, as you may probably recollect, an act had been passed by the Canadian parliament, providing that reciprocity in trade between that province and the U.S. should be established so soon as a corresponding act should have been adopted by Congress. To procure the passage of an act of this description through Congress was therefore the object of the friends of Reciprocity, both in the U.S. and in Canada. They represented to the Canadian Government that it was absolutely necessary that certain expenses should be incurred at Washington. The public mind, as they averred, had to be enlightened ; the press and legislature informed ; erroneous views removed. Mr.

Andrews directed this expenditure, and I think that
during the period which elapsed between 1849 and 1854
the Canadian government contributed about 10,000
dollars (£2,000) towards it.

" But little progress, as you know, was made during
these years, and when I proceeded to Washington in the
spring of 1854 by your orders, Mr. Andrews was engaged
in organizing a meeting of delegates from the provinces
to agree upon terms to be submitted to the Government
of the U.S.—a plan less likely to promote the objects
which it professed to have in view could not in my opinion
have been devised. Each delegate would have felt that
his popularity and honour depended upon the zeal and
stubbornness with which he sustained the extreme claims
of his own province. To imagine that such a body would
have agreed to propositions, which the Congress of the
U.S. would have accepted, was simply absurd. I re-
versed the process (you must pardon me for referring to
circumstances which although familiar to you are probably not so well known to Sir W. Molesworth), obtained
from the U.S. Government the best terms I could get, and
then gave the Colonial legislatures the option of accepting
or rejecting them. You know the result. The terms
were accepted almost by acclamation, and wherever
there was any disappointment, it was harmlessly vented
in abuse of the negotiator.

" Mr. A. evidently viewed my appearance at Washington with very little favour, and I was at first afraid
that he might give me some trouble. However, seeing
the turn which things were taking there, he soon reverted
to better sentiments, and professed to be as zealous as
ever in the cause. When Mr. Marcy had signed the
Treaty, I said to Mr. Crampton that as the credit of the
Government of the U.S. was now to a certain extent at

least engaged in procuring its passage through Congress, nothing as it appeared to me could be more injudicious than that either he or I should seem to meddle in the matter. In pursuance of this opinion, in which he entirely concurred, I left Washington by the first train after the Treaty had been signed.

" Mr. Andrews however remained behind, and during the interval which elapsed between the date of the signature of the Treaty, and that of the passage of the Act of Congress which ratified it, kept up a constant fire of letters and telegraphic messages detailing his exertions in the cause and the difficulties against which he had to contend.[1] I adhered to my rule of not answering these letters. But it was impossible to throw Mr. Andrews over altogether, as his hostility might have been dangerous, and in acknowledgment of his voluminous correspondence, one or two notes of encouragement were written to him by Mr. Ross, the exact purport of which he can explain.

" When the affair was over, I was anxious that Mr. Andrews, who had no doubt given himself a good deal of trouble, should be liberally dealt with, and after communicating with Mr. Perley of New Brunswick (now appointed Commissioner under the Treaty) who professed to be in his confidence, the Canadian Government paid over to the promoters of Reciprocity in New York, 10,000 more, in the hope that the sum would satisfy his claims. When I reached New York, however, on my way home, I met Andrews, who made representations to me somewhat similar to those which he appears to have made to the Nova Scotian Attorney-General (missing of course the ridiculous assertion that I had authorized him to pay 15,000 [2] to the Senate) respecting the liabilities which

[1] The letters are still in existence, a curious collection.
[2] Pounds, not dollars, in the preceding correspondence.

he had incurred in promoting the passage of the Reciprocity Act through Congress. He wished me to induce you to make some handsome contribution to cover these expenses. I told him as before that I positively declined to have any conversation with him on money matters ; and I further informed him through Mr. Ross that before I could move in the matter in any way he must satisfy the Canadian Government of the justice of his claims. He then dropped the subject, and set to work to persuade me that you would be greatly the gainer if you would employ him as your agent to give a wholesome direction to public opinion in the States on the subject of the war,[1] and of the relations between the U.S. and England generally. Mr. A. has written to me on the subject since I left, but I did not feel sufficiently sure of my man to think that I should be warranted in troubling you on the subject.

" I have furnished these details for your information, and that of Sir W. Molesworth. Whether anything is to be gained by taking the Governor of Nova Scotia into our confidence in this matter may I think be more than doubtful. I should be greatly rejoiced if Andrews' claims could be settled. As your Washington Treaty, which has relieved the North American fleet, and deprived Her Majesty's subjects in the British provinces of their only pretext for desiring annexation to the United States on commercial grounds, has cost, special mission and all included, only about £400, perhaps you might afford to give a helping hand. I do not know what was the price of the Ashburton Treaty, for which, although it was styled a capitulation, the thanks of Parliament were given, but I suspect that the difference will go far to satisfy Andrews. Meanwhile I have endeavoured to set before you as dis-

---

[1] The Crimean War.

tinctly as I can the nature of our relations with that gentleman. I must refer you to Mr. Hincks and Mr. Ross for further information respecting the present position of his claims."[1]

The scope and importance of the Reciprocity Treaty of 1854 cannot be better described than in the words of Elgin's own report to Clarendon, written before the joy of diplomatic battle had quite passed away.[2] It had provided for the admission, duty free, into one of the greatest and most rapidly rising markets of the world, of all the more important staple products of the British North American colonies, among them coal, timber, fish, grain and flour. In exchange the people of the United States had obtained certain rights of fishing and navigation, valued by them very highly, but the enjoyment of these privileges was certain to be attended by benefits rather than loss to the colonists, for the reciprocal advantages were bound to produce a more rapid improvement of Colonial resources not hitherto adequately developed. The negotiator was not exaggerating one whit the value of his finished work when he said :

" It is my deliberate opinion, founded on a knowledge of the condition of these Colonies derived from long residence in these quarters, that the favourable results of this Treaty, should it come into operation, will be found

---

[1] Elgin to Clarendon, 25 August, 1855.
[2] *Ibid.*, 12 June, 1854.

very far to exceed what its most sanguine supporters have ventured to anticipate."[1]

The concluding formal stages of the Treaty were carried through with the same speed and certainty which marked the whole transaction. By 3 August, Elgin was able to cable to the Foreign Office, " Reciprocity Treaty confirmed by Senate," and on 4 August, Crampton telegraphed to Clarendon, " Now complete." By 5 August the Treaty was an accepted part of United States legislation. There was little hesitation in the provinces. Canada gave effect to the measure on 23 September;[2] Prince Edward Island on 7 October ; New Brunswick on 3 November, and Nova Scotia on 13 December. Even Newfoundland entered by the middle of 1855 ; and till 1866 Reciprocity proved itself one of the most important causes of colonial prosperity. In 1852 colonial exports to the United States were valued at rather more than 7 million dollars. By 1860, to take a less sensational date than the closing year of the agreement, they were worth almost 22 million dollars ; while imports from the South had increased from a value of 10 million dollars to one of almost 24 millions. But figures are vague, and disputable. The actual human value of Elgin's achievement is perhaps

[1] Elgin to Clarendon, 12 June, 1854.
[2] It had passed through both houses on the preceding day.

better gauged by the letter which he received a fort-
night after the signing of the Treaty from a flour
miller, Jacob Keefer, in Western Canada :

" I have been watching with much anxiety the progress of the reciprocity negotiations. I was observant
of your Excellency's visit to Washington and I perceive
by the speeches at Portland how prominently reciprocity
stands out among the good things to come which they
there saw, and upon Mr. Merritt's return I was delighted
to learn from him that the question was in a much better
state than I had supposed it to be.

" My Welland Mills cost me eight thousand pounds—
I thought at the time I was justified in undertaking
respectably, but from the turn our trade took I was led
into a great deal of trouble by my too-confident enterprise. I have two sons in California, owing to that cause.
Now I believe reciprocity will be accomplished, and in
consequence of it I shall be enabled to effect the arrangements necessary for the recovery and occupation of my
mills, and to call home my sons, and employ them here,
which I greatly prefer.

" For this gratifying improvement in the state of a
measure in which I deem my own well-being so intimately
concerned, I feel as if I were personally indebted to your
Excellency, and though it is, no doubt, very unusual,
and perhaps very irregular, I nevertheless venture in this
manner to offer your Excellency my very sincere thanks."[1]

*   *   *   *   *

Before the winter of 1854 descended on Canada,
Lord Elgin had completed his programme of political and economic reforms and advances : and

[1] Jacob Keefer to Lord Elgin, 20 June, 1854.

no summary statement need repeat the detail furnished in these last two chapters. But in the correspondence, private and official, of the last months of office in Canada there may be noticed one unconscious evidence of his complete identification with the people over whom he ruled, and his sense that great quiet things had been accomplished. He had now spent seven years in his province, associating with Canada in dark days, as now in brighter. He had fought his enemies, who were also those of Canada, in such a fashion that reconciliation was always possible and natural. He had lived as a citizen of Montreal, and Toronto, and Quebec ; and in his many journeys he had touched the solid wholesome life of the countryside. To such a man, and in such a country, there was bound to come a time when it was not absurd to talk of the place as home. Indeed, had he only known it, his Canadian regime was to prove the longest period of settled life to be enjoyed by him when once he had left his youthful days behind. It was natural then that the quiet beautiful mornings of his last summer and the peace of his last Canadian autumn should bring something very like regret at the thought of departure, because they revealed to him the depth of affection with which he had come to regard his Government, his country, and his people. In June, 1854, he was just returning from a long leave in Britain and a crowded and exciting visit to the United States. It was Sunday, and fair weather, and as he quietly made his way in the morning to his Quebec home the kindly people of Quebec greeted him from their windows with nods of recognition, and one old lady whispered " Welcome home again."

" Never since I left," he wrote to Lady Elgin, who was in England, " have I seen anything so lovely : the trees clothed in tenderest green : the ships with their flags hanging motionless on the masts, and standing fixed like statues on the burnished mirror in which they were reflected. Not a breath of wind, yet a delightful refreshing coolness in the air : the whole scene bathed in a perfect ocean of light. . . . And so I have with my own hand severed the tie which bound me to this spot, to the interests which have so long engrossed me, and where any trouble or anxiety I may have had has been so amply compensated in the abundance of the return for the seed sown." [1]

Or, once more, in autumn. He had been travelling far and wide : from Quebec to Montreal ; Montreal to Buffalo ; Buffalo to Niagara Falls, and Toronto, and the Bay of Quinté. He had sailed down that exquisite water-way : had welcomed and been welcomed by his Kingston friends, and once more he was heading for Quebec on a St. Lawrence not yet spoiled by summer pleasure-houses.

[1] Letters to Lady Elgin, 12 June, 1854.

" We are at this moment," he records, " nearing the
Cedar Rapids under a perfectly calm sky ; a glowing sun
sinking in the West, and casting a mantle of fresh gold
over the wooded banks, which are already clothed in their
most brilliant autumnal colours. Shall I own that it is
with very mingled feelings that I have made this tour :
gratification at the evidences of improvement which I
have seen around me, and at the kindness of my reception, and sadness to think that it is a last visit. . . . I
cannot without a pang bring myself to believe that hence-
forth all the interests of this great and thriving country
are to be to me as a matter in which I have no concern.
Notwithstanding the atrocities of the press, it is impossible
for me to go through the country without feeling that I
have a strong hold on the people of the country ; that I
occupy a place here which no one ever filled before."[1]

There are two kinds of satisfaction with, acquiescence in, what one has done and been—one false,
the other true and accurate in its self-judgments.
As Elgin, in this mood, reflected in tranquillity on
his seven Canadian years, he was judging with
strict truthfulness the work he had done, and the
simplest verdict on that work is his own : " I
occupy a place here which no one ever filled
before."

[1] Letters to Lady Elgin, 7 October, 1854.

CHAPTER V

THE FIRST MISSION TO CHINA
AND JAPAN, 1857-59

BETWEEN 1855 and 1857 occurred the first and longest of three brief intervals in Lord Elgin's otherwise continuous services overseas. All of these intervals present the same characteristics, and in all of them it is apparent that the choice of career had now been made irrevocably for administrative not parliamentary work. In 1855 Lord Elgin made one most important decision, that he would not oppose the Whig Government which now had Palmerston at its head. Like most of his fellow-Peelites he occupied a difficult position, for it is always an invidious thing to change one's party, and yet men trained under Peel found it difficult to regard the Earl of Derby and Benjamin Disraeli as wise guides towards an intelligently and honestly conservative policy. At the same time Elgin had the best of reasons for showing friendliness to Palmerston's party. On questions of public policy he found himself generally in agreement with Whig views; and Palmerston had recognized this agreement by offering him the Duchy of Lancaster shortly after his return from Canada. The Whigs, and more especially Earl Grey, had been as loyal friends and defenders of his various Canadian policies, as the Tories had been critical. But, in 1855, the decisive argument in his mind leading him to support Palmerston, although in some things he still maintained an attitude of friendly neutrality, was that the Crimean War called for the banishment of merely party views. " It appeared to me," Lord Elgin said in his speech on the resolutions on the war in Russia, " to be the bounden duty of every patriotic man who had not some very valid or substantial reason to assign for adopting a contrary course, to tender a frank and generous support to the government of the Queen."[1] It was as natural for Elgin, as it had been for the Duke of Wellington, to take a national, rather than a partisan, view in a great crisis. Early in 1856 Lord Elgin once more appeared in politics, to clarify the military situation in Canada and, through Canada, with reference to the United States.[2] But the impression given during these two years is that of one who has for the time ceased to function in his proper sphere,

[1] Parliamentary Debates, 14 May, 1855.
[2] Ibid., 17 April, 27 May, 1856.

and who is slow to accept the conditions exacted from all who wish to shine in parliament. Three years later Lord Granville made a shrewd comment on him that he " doubted his ever being much use in parliament."[1] For the rest, he spent much time with his family, over the business of the estate, and in visiting old friends, especially in Scotland ; with, now and then, the mild excitement of such public appearances as when Glasgow offered him its freedom. His career resumed its normal direction and progress only when affairs in China suddenly flared up into what looked like a new Chinese war ; and the Government, after having approached the Duke of Newcastle, offered Elgin the headship of a most important mission to China and Japan.[2]

From the spring of 1857, with one break of some ten months down to the end of 1860, Lord Elgin was actually engaged in rectifying the relations between Great Britain and the Chinese Empire.[3] It is an error, easily made but nevertheless disastrously misleading, to think of the work of these

[1] Fitzmaurice, *Life of Lord Granville* : Granville to Canning, 10 August, 1859.

[2] The Duke of Argyll declares that Newcastle was the first choice of the Cabinet : *Autobiography and Memoirs*, II, p. 75.

[3] Three volumes of correspondence relative to China and presented to the House of Commons have special reference to this subject : *Papers relating to the proceedings of H.M. Naval*

years as originating in a half-discreditable episode
connected with a small Chinese trading vessel at
Canton. The story of the lorcha *Arrow*, and of how
Sir John Bowring, Consul Parkes, and Sir Michael
Seymour levied war on the Chinese government,
is only one surface indication of a primary problem
in the world-politics of the nineteenth century—
the fate of China. The Manchu dynasty there was
not merely alien to China, but, after exhibiting
genuine capacity for governing in the seventeenth
and eighteenth centuries, it had begun to betray
the signs, so unmistakable in Eastern despotisms,
of incurable decadence. Apart from the imperfect
control by the centre of the outlying parts, the
growth of secret societies throughout China, and
the inextinguishable disorders of the Tai-ping rebellion indicated that Manchu rule at Peking must
either reform its ways or cease to exist. Nothing,
indeed, but the endless patience of the Chinese
kept the Empire in political existence.

But the fate of China depended on more than
Manchu administration. Parallel with the expan-

Forces at Canton (1857), here called China Corr. I ; *Correspondence
relative to the Earl of Elgin's special missions to China and Japan*
(1859), here called China Corr. II ; and *Correspondence respecting affairs in China, 1859–60* (1861), here called China
Corr. III. The copy of the earliest of the three blue-books
used by me belonged to Harry Parkes, and contains a few of
his markings.

sion of peoples like the British and French overseas had gone the even greater expansion of European trade, and in the train of the traders conquest and European colonization were natural attendants. The strife between Britain and China which had ended in the treaties of 1842 and 1843 had been something much more significant than a quarrel over opium. It had intimated to China that the expansive, or, as some called them, the predatory nations of the West, Britain, France, the United States, with Russia as an Oriental partner, were beginning to interest themselves in the future of a country which might provide new territory, subjects, and trade profits, for countries whose greed should prove stronger than their consciences. The ultimate fate of China is even now obscure, but Lord Elgin's two missions, combined as they were with similar and simultaneous action by France, the United States, and Russia, decided that whatever else might happen, the partition of China should be ruled out of account, and that, in order to prevent the advent of *casus belli* likely to tempt European powers to territorial aggression, the Peking government must not only accept responsibility for the acts of its provincial administrators, but open its gates without any hesitation to a trade which would take no refusal, and administer treaties in a spirit of honour and truth.

The immediate cause of trouble in 1856, stated as fairly as possible, was this.

By the treaties of 1842 and 1843, the five ports of Canton, Foochow, Amoy, Ningpo and Shanghai had been thrown open, British subjects and their families being guaranteed against molestation or restraint. Nevertheless at Canton, not only had the region open to foreigners been severely restricted and fixed outside the city, but every difficulty was placed in the way of personal communications between the British and the Chinese authorities at that city, which was for European trade purposes then the capital of China. Further the means of communication with the central government were, and were meant by the Chinese authorities to be, entirely denied to the foreign trading powers. Thus in case of trouble not only was there the maximum of difficulty in settling local disputes at Canton, but also the minimum chance of calling in Peking to rectify the injustices inflicted at the Southern port.

By the treaty of 1843, an additional article [1] had

[1] Article XVII. The scope of the article was extended by a Hong-Kong ordinance making it lawful " for Chinese residents within this colony to apply for and obtain colonial registration, provided the person or persons applying as owners be registered lessees of Crown lands within this colony." For the validity of this ordinance see the discussions in the Houses of Lords and Commons, 24 and 26 February, 26 and 27 February, 2 and 3 March, 1857. I confess to thinking Palmerston's attitude in the affair correct.

been introduced to regulate the local shipping traffic round Hong-Kong, Canton and Macao, and certain "small vessels belonging to the English nation, called schooners, cutters, lorchas, etc." were, for the convenience of both sides, compelled to register themselves and fulfil certain fixed conditions. It is useless, as Lord Palmerston's opponents did in both Lords and Commons, in 1857, to discuss whether the conditions of the treaty and the local ordinance which defined its operation in Hong-Kong conformed to those of the British Merchant Shipping legislation, or what the exact relationship between the mariners of these small craft and the Chinese government was. To simplify trade, and presumably to prevent smuggling, Britain and China consented to this regulation ; and the authorities at Hong-Kong had legislated to simplify the local working of the new arrangements.

Under these conditions, a lorcha called the *Arrow* was seized at Canton by the Chinese officials, her British flag lowered, and, on the pretext of certain of the crew having once been pirates on another craft, all but two of the crew were carried off. The *Arrow* had had a romantic past, once having been captured by pirates, and then being recaptured, and later sold by " braves " belonging to a loyalist association. But on 8 October she was entirely respectable and law-abiding in all but one particular—her registration had terminated on 27 September. In the interval, however, she had been absent from the port of registration, Hong-Kong, and as, in any case, the Chinese authorities plainly did not know of the irregularity, that fact could not be pled in excuse of a clear violation of treaty regulations, aggravated by an insult to the British flag.

The immediate consequence of this measure, which had been authorized by the local Governor-General Yeh, was that the British representative at Hong-Kong, Sir John Bowring, moved by the British Consul at Canton, Harry Parkes, called in the services of the British admiral in these parts, Sir Michael Seymour, and started what in any other empire but that of China would have been war with the offending authorities, shelling and capturing ports, and shelling and entering the city of Canton. All this was the *reductio ad absurdum* of a national policy which refused to keep treaty agreements, refused to accept obvious commercial facts, which stimulated local authorities both to disallow treaty conditions, and to refuse frank communication with complaining parties ; and which imagined that in the modern world a great power (for such China considered herself) could be at war with another power locally, and yet at peace with the same power everywhere else outside the disturbed district. Further, lest it be thought that the British action was unique, the United States authorities, only a few days later, were compelled to answer an even more aggravated insult to their flag and their subjects, by shelling and utterly destroying some of the forts guarding the river at Canton.

In what followed the three dominant figures were Harry Parkes, Lord Palmerston, and, as Lord Palmerston's plenipotentiary, Lord Elgin. Sir John Bowring figured largely and unfortunately in the parliamentary discussions ; but Bowring was a " slight " man, dominated by too high a sense of his own importance, and yet without stubbornness and resolution to maintain the risky game which he had started. Parkes as well as Elgin counted little on him, although for some months, late in 1856 and early in 1857, he figures largely in correspondence. He soon disappeared from the scene as an embarrassed phantom.

But Harry Parkes was a very different man ; engaged almost from childhood in Chinese work, resolute, clearheaded, extremely unsentimental when it came to business, although fair and just and almost uncannily well-informed in the ways of Chinese officials, and in the methods by which they sought to evade their obligations. As the Chinese

themselves confessed, this was Parkes', not Bowring's affair, and Parkes regulated his conduct,
which he also meant to be the policy of Britain,
by the following line of argument.

Firstly the act of Commissioner Yeh in invading
the *Arrow*, arresting the crew, and lowering the
flag, was but a single example of what the Chinese
government, and more especially Yeh, had been
consistently attempting for years—to undo the work
of 1842 and 1843, and to diminish to a vanishing
point foreign trade and liberties in Canton. It
must therefore be cancelled by the complete dis-
avowal of what had been done, and by a perfectly
full and official apology. That remedy was refused
by Yeh, and not even the shelling of all the forts,
and the entrance into Canton of British naval
forces, could affect the stolid resistance of the
Commissioner.

So Sir Michael Seymour proceeded to expound
the second argument of the indomitable consul at
Canton.

" To prevent the recurrence of evils like the present,"
he wrote to the High Commissioner on 27 October,
" which have been occasioned by the disregard paid by
the Imperial Commissioner to the repeated application
for redress and satisfaction made to him by letter in the
matter of the *Arrow*, by H.M. Plenipotentiary and the
Consul—writing in consequence of the closing of the city
to foreigners, by the only means of communication—*I*

*demanded for all foreign representatives the same free access to
the authorities and city of Canton (where all the Chinese high
officials reside) as is enjoyed under Treaty at the other four ports,
and denied to us at Canton alone.*"[1]

When the " City Question," as it was called,
only evoked more subtleties and evasions on the
part of Yeh, and was met by the same policy of
masterly inactivity, and when news arrived by the
British mail (of 20 March) that Lord Elgin had
been appointed to deal, as British Plenipotentiary,
with the whole question, Parkes naturally moved
to his third position. " Canton," he wrote to a
friend in Hong-Kong, " must fall. I see no hope
of any arrangement being arrived at without this
primary step being effected ; but I do trust that
with the fall of that city—a punishment upon it
long wanted—hostilities may end, *and that the
Emperor may then consent to receive a representative at
Peking.*"[2]

It is possible to hold that Parkes was too completely dominated by the facts immediately in front
of him, and that he was the very incarnation of
" the man on the spot." It is certain, also, that
he showed no reluctance over involving England
in hostilities with China. As a " sinologue " he

[1] Sir M. Seymour to the Secretary to the Admiralty, 14
November, 1856.
[2] Lane Poole, *Life of Sir Harry Parkes*, I, pp. 262–3.

was at first included by Lord Elgin in the distrust
which the ambassador showed towards all the men
on the spot. But Elgin, as Palmerston before him,
could not but see the amazing soundness, tinged of
course with audacity, in his subordinate's policy ;
and the final settlement of 1860 was not unlike the
project which Parkes must have cherished from the
very start of troubles in 1856.

Before passing to the beginning of the mission of
1857, the attitude of the British Prime Minister
deserves a brief description. Palmerston was following something more deeply considered than a
policy of blustering patriotism. It is advisable
here, as in some other regions, not to under-rate
the wisdom of Palmerstonian policy at its best. As
Foreign Secretary Palmerston had always been
resolute in his defence of British subjects abroad,
but in the long-drawn-out correspondence with the
Chinese over the Canton question,[1] he had acted
with cool judgment. Even when the Chinese
Commissioner at Canton had turned his back on
an explicit promise to open Canton to the British
two years from the date of the conference with Sir
John Davis in 1847, Palmerston advised his agent
to delay his assertion of the claim, and to await
some better occasion. He was reluctant to over-
turn by any rash action British prosperity and

[1] China Corr. I, appendix A.

Chinese peace.[1] He seized the opportunity of Parkes' home leave to see him in London in 1850 ; and the information which he then gained seems to have strengthened in his mind the view that the right of entrance into Canton was the key of the whole difficulty.[2] Still, no action was taken.

It is not unfair to either man to say that in their different spheres, Palmerston and Parkes thought in similar terms about China ; although the compromises, which the British Foreign Minister's wider view of British policy, and his fear of possible European complications naturally suggested, were criticized by Parkes as too reluctant and uncertain, to produce a good effect on China. It was comparatively easy for Palmerston, when the whole matter came up for discussion in both Lords and Commons, in February and March, 1857, not only to back his men, and accept responsibility for what they had done, but, much more naturally than any other speaker on both sides, to take a realistic and practical view of the situation. His actions were even more eloquent than his speeches. Defeated after a most important debate in the House of Commons by 16 votes, he never for one moment

[1] China Corr. I, p. 191 : Palmerston to Bonham, 25 June, 1849.
[2] *Life of Sir H. Parkes*, I, p. 145.

faltered. He wished, he said, in declaring his policy prior to an appeal to the country,[1] " to maintain in China, as elsewhere, security for the lives and property of British subjects ; to maintain the rights of this country as arising out of treaty obligations ; to endeavour by negotiations either to improve our existing relations or to restore amicable relations if events have brought about a rupture." " There will be no change, and can be no change in the policy of the government with respect to events in China "—a bold challenge to a house fresh from voting against that policy. But this was not bluff ; it was confidence based on a really sound understanding of the Chinese problem. He was not above taking a hint from his chief opponent. Cobden himself, as soon as he had been convinced that Palmerston's intentions were unchanged, and that the country was likely to support a firm policy, gave him some sound advice :

" Send out a competent person by this very steamer [2] armed with full authority to represent the Executive government at home ; let him supersede all the existing authorities in China, and give him distinct instructions to act according as the state of things which he finds when he gets there may seem to require."[3]

---

[1] 5 March, 1857.

[2] This would have involved departure from London on 8 March.

[3] Parliamentary Debates, 5 March, 1857.

That, although with rather less abrupt haste than Cobden desired, was exactly what Palmerston did. For, concurrently with the close of the parliamentary session, Lord Elgin's appointment as High Commissioner and Plenipotentiary was made known. His commission gave him liberal powers, and with the true Palmerston touch he was bidden to secure

" the assent of the Chinese government to the residence at Pekin, or to the occasional visit to that capital, at the option of the British Government, of a minister duly accredited by the Queen to the Emperor of China, and the recognition of the right of the British Plenipotentiary and Chief Superintendent of Trade to communicate directly in writing with the high officers at the Chinese capital, and to send his communications by messengers of his own selection ; such arrangements affording the best means of securing the due execution of the existing treaties, and of preventing future misunderstandings." [1]

Before April ended, then, Lord Elgin had set out on a task which was to occupy his time and energy for practically four years, and his success in which laid the foundation for all subsequent English dealings with China. His mission was to be supported by force, troops being ordered from England, Mauritius, and Singapore, to co-operate with Seymour's ships : it was to be conducted in harmony with a similar mission to be despatched simultaneously

[1] China Corr. II, p. 3.   I retain the old spelling, Pekin, in the documents which use that form.

by Napoleon III ; and during the period Sir John
Bowring's functions in China were to remain in
abeyance. Additional zest was given to the work
by a paragraph instructing the plenipotentiary,
after Chinese troubles had been settled, to proceed
to Japan and " to enter into negotiations with the
government of that country."[1]

After an uneventful voyage to India, the Chinese
mission entered a region of storms from which it
was not to escape for a full twelvemonth. At
Point de Galle in Ceylon, Ashburnham, who was
to be commander of the troops in China, brought
Elgin news of the outbreak of the Indian Mutiny.
That happened on 26 May, and till September the
chief centre of interest was Calcutta, not Canton.
Elgin's first impulse was to hurry through with the
Chinese affair before the influence of Indian news
could work harm, and then " to place the regiments destined for China at the disposal of Government for service elsewhere."[2] With this in view
he and Ashburnham set out. At Penang there was
no news at all about India ; but at Singapore
urgent letters from Canning forced him to send out
orders to the 5th Regiment, on its way from Mauritius, and the 90th from England, to carry on direct
to Calcutta. That was only the beginning of com-

[1] China Corr. II, p. 6.
[2] Letters to Lady Elgin, 27 May, 1857.

plications. Arriving at Hong-Kong without the main land force on which he counted, Elgin found that there was no news of the co-operating French mission, and that the representative of the United States on the spot had no special instructions. He would have to act, if immediate action were necessary, in isolation. But isolated action was almost impossible. His military and naval experts told him that there was not a sufficiency of troops in Hong-Kong for operations against Canton. If he proceeded towards Peking, he was almost certain to meet with a rebuff, and in that case he had no force to use at the one point where action then would become necessary, Canton. Meanwhile his prestige as plenipotentiary must suffer ; and India was sinking deeper and deeper into troubles. Lord Elgin's action in this emergency is one of the most notable and admirable things in his career, and he must be allowed to tell his own story :

" Will you think me mad, or what will your view of my proceedings be ? Here I am actually on my way to Calcutta. To Calcutta ! you will exclaim in surprise. The reasons for this step are so numerous, that I can hardly attempt to enumerate them. I found myself at Hong-Kong without troops and without competent representatives of our allies to concert with. Doomed either to *aborder* the Court of Pekin alone, without the power of acting vigorously, if I met a repulse, or to spend three months at Hong-Kong doing nothing and proclaiming

to the whole world that I am waiting for the Frenchmen
—I considered the great objections which existed to either
of these courses. *Sur ces entrefaites* came further letters
from Canning begging for more help from me, and showing that things are even worse with him than they were
when I first heard from him. It occurred to me that I
might occupy the three months well in running up to Calcutta, taking with me what assistance I can collect for
him, and learning from him what chance I have of getting
before the winter the troops which I have detached for
his support." [1]

This fresh support cost him the very heart of
what was left of his armed mission. It meant Captain Peel and the two ships *Shannon* and *Pearl* ; it
included even some 300 marines who had just
arrived at Hong-Kong from England. Elgin had
organized what became famous in its day as Peel's
Naval Brigade. And he did all this without
possessing any clear information on Indian needs,
and in direct defiance of his instructions. At Singapore, on his way to Calcutta, urgent and gloomy
letters from Canning confirmed him in his judgment ; but it must be remembered that the decision
had been made long before he received these decisive documents from India ; and indeed he had
also given orders that the 23rd and 82nd Regiments, on their way to China from England, should
also be diverted. When he arrived in Calcutta,

[1] Letters to Lady Elgin, 19 July, 1857.

he was a plenipotentiary indeed, but with nothing more at his disposal in China than the 59th, which was then in garrison, and in very indifferent condition.[1] Never was independent action more fully justified. Even if the Chinese venture should be indefinitely postponed, as it was not, the influence of the fresh troops on the situation was astonishing. Writing from Calcutta on 26 August, he was able to tell Lady Elgin that " General Havelock, who commands (on the Lucknow relief expedition), says he can do nothing unless he gets the 5th and 90th Regiments (the two I sent from Singapore on my own responsibility). The men of the *Pearl* and *Shannon* and the marines are guarding Calcutta, or on their way up to Allahabad," and Peel's 68-pounders had a very large part to play in operations. What a bystander thought of the transaction, was shown in a timely and courteous note from the Governor of Ceylon :

" You may think me impertinent in volunteering an opinion upon what in the first instance only concerns you and the Queen and Lord Canning. But having seen something of public life during a great part of my own, which is now fast verging into the ' sere and yellow leaf,' I may venture to say that I never knew a nobler thing than that which you have done, in preferring the safety of India to the success of your Chinese negotiations.
" If I know anything of English public opinion, this

---

[1] Elgin to Clarendon, 22 August, 1857.

single act will place you higher in general estimation as a statesman than your whole past career, honourable and fortunate as it has been. For it is not every man who would venture to alter the destination of a force, upon the despatch of which a parliament has been dissolved, and a government might have been superseded. It is not every man who would consign himself for many months to political inaction in order simply to serve the interests of his country. You have set a bright example at a moment of darkness and calamity, and if India can be saved, it is to you that we shall owe its redemption, for nothing short of the Chinese expedition would have supplied the means of holding our ground until further reinforcements are received."[1]

Conscious of virtue, but denuded of armed force, Elgin left Calcutta, no longer on a warship, but on a merchant vessel, reaching once more the proper scene of action late in September—once more to find that the French and American representatives had not even yet arrived, while his military colleague commanded " a whole lot of doctors and staff, and officers of all kinds without any troops." In the words of Yeh, the Chinese Commissioner, who must have had some sense of humour, " Elgin passes day after day at Hong-Kong, stamping his foot and sighing."[2]

On the eve of the events which carried Lord

[1] Sir H. Ward to Lord Elgin ; from a copy in Lady Elgin's writing described as of " August, 1857—Ceylon."
[2] China Corr. II, pp. 221–2.

Elgin almost to the gates of Peking, it is well to describe exactly the mood in which he approached his work, for so far was he from adopting the Anglo-Chinese point of view, expressed in 1857 by men like Harry Parkes, that from first to last he had to meet much bitter local criticism.

He had no sympathy with the immediate cause of troubles. " Nothing," he told his wife, " could be more contemptible than the origin of our existing quarrel," and he thought the *Arrow* question " a scandal to us."[1] His first impressions of the Europeans in China were very unfavourable. He thought that they were afraid of the Chinese and therefore " very bloody " ; that their *idée fixe* was that there should be a general massacre at Canton ; and that, apart altogether from his own countrymen, he was about to secure liberties for European nations which many of them would shamefully misuse. He found the Chinese peaceful, industrious, and often pathetically friendly even to his military expedition, whatever their Governors might be ; and everywhere, in his private letters, his despatches, and his official speeches, he revealed a mood of moderation and merciful justice which was unwelcome to the local fire-eaters. He told the Shanghai merchants that " Christian civiliz-

[1] Letters to Lady Elgin, 24 December, and 9 December, 1857.

ation will have to win its way among a sceptical and ingenious people by making it manifest that a faith which reaches to Heaven furnishes better guarantees for public and private morality than one which does not rise above the earth " ; and he warned the missionaries that while it was natural for them to look exclusively to the benefits attaching to the extension of European rights, it was his painful duty to take precautions lest these be abused.[1] He never shirked the awkward facts which pioneer commerce always creates in its early efforts among strange peoples ; and, knowing too well what Dutch and Portuguese history in the East had revealed of shame and wrong, he feared the consequences of his own possible success. So prominently is this temper of moderation and mercy illustrated in his letters and despatches during the first Chinese mission, that the question naturally rises whether it was not a false charity, opening the way for Manchu bad faith, and so to the necessity for re-doing in 1860 what had been wrongly done in 1858. That certainly would have been—nay was—the view of so competent a critic as Harry Parkes. But the criticism is not merely unjust ; it is unworthy of the better traditions of the British Empire. It may be granted, as Elgin recognized,

[1] Both of these speeches were in March, 1858. See China Corr. II.

that with so extraordinary a government as that of Peking, arrogant without any knowledge of its actual position in the world, incurably false, and violent as only weakness can be violent, the most merciful policy was that of the strong hand. But not even sheer unrestrained force in 1858 could have averted the ill-faith which involved the necessity of a second mission and the seizure of Peking in 1860. Lord Elgin was thinking in very broad terms, and his views embraced considerations, important even to the fire-eaters, although beyond their limited vision. If Christian ethics have any place in politics, they must govern the first contacts of Christendom with the non-Christian world. It was impossible for an English gentleman to deal with the Chinese people as though the gospels had never been written and accepted as the standards of English conduct. Even on a less exalted plane, the future relations between Europe and China could be profitable and decent on both sides, only if the conquering west should exhibit that same willingness to accept limits and avoid excess which kept Europe itself, except under Napoleon, and until 1914, from absolute disaster in diplomacy. Further, Lord Elgin had in the first place to consider that, should his moderation be consistently maintained, the quarrel with the Manchu emperor need not (as actually it did not) involve more of

China in strife than the locality where trouble had arisen, and the centre which gave support to the offenders ; and, in the second place, he knew that a very little excess of force would send the whole central government toppling over in hopeless ruin and that, whatever misguided enthusiasts might say, the possibility of a successful Tai-ping advance on Peking was something which no friend, either of China, or of the European communities there, could contemplate without horror.

If, then, the narrative of Elgin's dealings with Canton and Peking, which follows, may seem to accept Elgin's own standpoint of moderation rather than the drastic counsels of the Anglo-Chinese community, it is because his policy of mercy, mixed with judgment, was in accordance not only with ordinary christian maxims, but with Machiavelli's acknowledgment that there is a place in statescraft for benevolence.

The story of the first Chinese mission falls into clearly marked episodes, the capture and government of Canton, the advance towards Peking, the treaty of Tientsin, the visit to Japan, and the revision of the Chinese tariff. It begins with the return from India on 20 September, 1857, and ends with the departure of the mission from the Canton river in March, 1859.

The other principals in the affair arrived in the

South between the middle of October and 18 November ; first Baron Gros for France, then Reed for the United States, and finally the Russian ambassador who came to Hong-Kong after a double rebuff at Kiakhta and Peking. Early in December, the allied plans were complete, and a letter was despatched to Commissioner Yeh demanding the execution at Canton of all treaty engagements, including free admission of Europeans into Canton, and compensation for losses sustained during the late disturbances.[1] The original period of warning, six days, lengthened to twenty-six, but Yeh remained obdurate. His happiest touch of unconscious humour in reply was a suggestion that as, among earlier British agents, Davis had earned recall by his vigour, Bonham the " title of Wei-li-pa "[2] by surrender, it was " doubtless the duty of your Excellency to imitate the conduct of the Pleni-potentiary Bonham."[3] A line of allied ships an-chored in front of Canton, and, on 28 December, the attack was made and succeeded with perfect ease. A week later, Yeh fell into the hands of his old enemy Harry Parkes, and the allies, Russia and the United States counting as observant neutrals, found themselves with the government of the Can-

[1] Elgin to Commissioner Yeh, 12 December, 1857.
[2] Presumably his baronetcy.
[3] Yeh to Elgin, 14 December, 1857.

ton district in their reluctant hands. The military operations had been simple to the verge of farce ; the real crux lay in reorganizing the local administration. It was plain that the city must be retained as a counter in later negotiations in the north, and Elgin at once took active steps. " It is indispensable," he wrote to the allied chiefs,[1] " that a government *de facto* should be at once established." So a curious joint government, partly allied commissioners of whom Harry Parkes was the compelling spirit, partly Chinese authorities with the local governor and Tartar general at their head, was set up, and functioned admirably until the time came for its withdrawal four years later. It was part of the grim humour of the situation that the state instalment of the new administration on 9 January was delayed because instructions had not been sent to the sentry who guarded the Chinese Governor and general, and he had refused to let them leave the room in which they were confined.[2] It was high time that some control should be established, for the allied troops, and especially the French, had become disorderly ; and Elgin hinted plainly to the others that if this were not stopped, he would consider evacuation.[3] The presiding

[1] 30 December, 1857.
[2] Letters to Lady Elgin, 10 January, 1858.
[3] *Ibid.*, 16 January ; 20 January, 1858.

217

genius of the new government was unmistakably Harry Parkes whose reports to the plenipotentiary convey a strong impression of energy and judgment. The sale of liquor was interdicted, a patrol, chiefly of English soldiers, kept order, proclamations informed the population of the will of the governors, and, when the blockade which had extinguished the trade of Canton was lifted, Parkes was able to report that already, by April, eight million pounds of tea had been purchased and the price paid partly in imported cotton and cotton goods.

By that time the allied missions had moved north. Elgin's plan was to send beforehand a letter to Peking demanding direct negotiation with a plenipotentiary duly accredited by the Emperor of China, who should present himself at Shanghai before the end of March. Then, should that be refused, he meant to push quickly to the north, and dictate terms as near the capital as possible, probably at Tientsin. To support his diplomacy he desired the admirals to back him, especially with all the light craft under their command—there would be river work on the Peiho requiring that kind of vessel.

But in Chinese diplomacy, if Europe proposes, Asia indisposes, and Chinese procrastination was assisted by a lamentable absence of energy in those who directed the armed forces. Laurence Oliphant, whose description of all these things is not only very charming but very accurate,[1] delivered the note, for despatch to Peking, at Soochow ; but the answer received on 30 March, was a complete *non possumus*, on the ground that between the officials of the Celestial Empire and the foreigners there must be no intercourse ; and that it would behove the English minister to wait in the South, and there make his arrangements locally, as no Imperial Commissioner ever conducted business at Shanghai.[2] It was, for Peking, quite beside the point that the treaties of 1842 and 1843 had specifically defined and legalized the forms of intercourse between the court and the Western powers. The occasion had now arrived for the exertion of pressure on the Peiho, and towards Peking ; and here the mission found another cause of delay—the British admiral had not fulfilled his promise of adequate armed support. The letters and despatches of the moment leave no doubt of Lord Elgin's disappointment and chagrin.

" I requested *officially* and he (the admiral) promised *officially* to send up here all the gunboats drawing little water which he could spare. He sends only one or two ; and instead of sailing on the 16th from Hong-Kong, as he

[1] The judgment is that of Harry Parkes.

[2] The Governor-General of the Two Kiang, and the Governor of Kiang-su to Lord Elgin, 21 March, 1858.

also promised to do, puts off his departure, without giving me any reason for it to the 23rd."

On 24 April he reported that the Admiral had arrived and left all his gunboats behind him, and on 29 April, with a touch of wrathful jest he gives the climax : " The flag of France is at this moment represented by two gunboats *within the bar of the Peiho river* ; that of England by two despatch-boats *on the top of it, aground.*"[1]

It was only the later helpless collapse of Chinese resistance which gave the episode this whimsical aspect. The French and English missions were now approaching the sea-gate to Peking, to extort conditions which the government there had hitherto absolutely refused. Armed resistance seemed almost certain ; or, if it was to be avoided, it would be avoided only by a brave preliminary display of force ; and the point against which force should be threatened must obviously be the forts at Taku, at the mouth of the river. So far as either the ambassadors or the admirals knew, resistance might have to be encountered there and a defeat, or, as seemed now more probable, a fiasco, would be fatal to the objects of the mission.

" Diplomacy simple is intelligible," Elgin wrote to Cumming Bruce, " war out and out is intelligible. Pot-

---

[1] From letters to Lady Elgin during April, 1858.

tinger had to do with the latter state of affairs. He had specific demands to prefer on the Chinese government, and orders to go on fighting, till they were granted. But the kind of armed diplomacy which I am instructed to wield is an absurdity unless the material force is directed by those who *ex animo* support the policy of the diplomat. The last folly committed by the admiral is his sending away Cresswell last night with one of the few vessels which can ascend the river. I made an effort to prevent this but failed."[1]

Even before this letter was despatched however, a new phase in operations had begun, and the complete absence of fighting power in the forts at Taku had saved Sir Michael Seymour and the allied missions from a position of stalemate. On 1 May the diplomats had instructed the sailors to clear the way, and prove to the Chinese government that England and France were in earnest; and in spite of naval slackness, the forts fell on 20 May.

" The Chinese had had (thanks to the admirals) several weeks to prepare, and their *morale* was greatly raised by our hesitations and delays. The poor fellows even stood at their guns, and fired away pretty steadily. But as they hardly ever hit, it is of very little consequence how much they fire. As soon as our men landed they abandoned the forts and ran off in all directions. We have hardly had any loss, I believe; but the French, who blundered a good deal with their gunboats, and then

---

[1] Elgin to Cumming Bruce, 22 May, 1858.

contrived to get blown up by setting fire to a powder-magazine, have suffered pretty severely. I fancy that we have got almost all the artillery which the Chinese Emperor possesses in this quarter."[1]

This decisive blow was quickly followed up by a further advance. The Chinese system of evading the main issue was never more clearly illustrated in its futility, and its consequences of humiliations to the Imperial Government, than at this stage. In April, three imperfectly accredited agents, Tau, Tsung, and Wu, had endeavoured to stave off a real negotiation, and they had protested in a helpless way that " the ascent of the river by British ships was extremely improper." But the British and French missions pushed relentlessly on to Tientsin, where they dropped anchor " at the point of junction of the grand canal and the Peiho River, in a most favourable position, therefore, for putting an arrest on the movements of the grain junks which bear tribute to Peking."[2] The consequence of the new threat, even before it was consummated, was that an imperial decree appointed Kweiliang, Chief Secretary of State, and Hwashana, President of the Board of Civil Office, to carry on the argument. But still the Chinese temporized. The new commissioners did not bring with them the

[1] Letters to Lady Elgin, 21 May, 1858.
[2] Elgin to Malmesbury, 1 June, 1858.

Kwan-fang, or official seal for Imperial Commissioners ; and by one of those startling exhibitions of oriental subtlety by which the Peking
government so regularly tried to thwart European
business, there was attached to the commission
the old commissioner, Kiyang, who had helped to
settle affairs in 1842—now " 72 years of age, and
apparently much broken ; walking and even
standing with difficulty, and very blind."[1] It
was a cruel " dodge," by which in some inexplicable
way negotiations were to be held up, and it ended,
unfortunately for the poor victim, in failure and in
an imperial order to Kiyang to commit suicide.
Meanwhile Elgin and Gros were grappling with
Kweiliang and Hwashana, the real ambassadors.
Elgin began the argument with a demonstration of
displeasure.

" I made up my mind," he reported to Lady Elgin,[2]
" disgusting as the part is to me, to act the rôle of the
' uncontrollably fierce barbarian,' as we are designated
in some of the confidential reports to the Chinese government which have come into our hands. These stupid
people, though they cannot resist, and hardly ever make
a serious attempt to do so, never yield anything except
under the influence of fear. . . . They said that they
had received the Emperor's orders to come down to treat
of our affairs. I answered that although I was much

[1] China Corr. II, pp. 320–3 : interview of Wade and Lay
with the Chinese.
[2] 5 June, 1858.

grieved by the neglect of the Prime Minister to answer the letters I had addressed to him, yet as they had on their cards stated that they had ' full powers,' I had consented to have this interview in order that we might compare our powers, and see whether we could treat together. I told them that I had brought mine, and I at once exhibited them, giving them a translation of the documents. They said that they had not powers of the same kind, but a decree of the Emperor appointing them, and they brought out a letter which was wrapped up in a sheet of yellow paper. . . . I thought the terms of this document rather ambiguous, besides which I was desirous to produce a certain effect ; so when it had been translated to me, I said that I was not sufficiently satisfied with it to be able to say on the spot whether I could treat with them or not. That I would, if they pleased, take a copy of it and consider the matter, but that I would not enter upon business with them at present. So saying I rose, moved to the front of the stage and ordered the escort to move and the chairs to be brought. This put the poor people into a terrible fluster. They made great efforts to induce me to sit down again, but I acted the part of the ' uncontrollably fierce ' to perfection, and set off for my abode. I had hardly reached it when I received two cards from my poor mandarins, thanking me for having gone so far as to meet them, etc."

Thanks to Laurence Oliphant's notes and photographs it is possible to visualize these two excellent Chinese gentlemen, with whom the mission had so much to do, and whose signatures are attached to the Magna Carta of English trade in China : Kweiliang " a venerable man of placid and benevolent expression, with a countenance full of intelligence although his eye was somewhat dimmed and his hand palsied from extreme age : " Hwashana " a younger man with a square, solid face, and a large nose " reminding Oliphant of the pictures of Oliver Cromwell.[1] Even after this exhibition of uncontrollable ferocity, events did not move quite smoothly, for first the envoys hedged on what they had seemed prepared to give, and then, through the Russian and American ministers, they tried to move Elgin's pity by representing that should they consent to the residence of ministers, at the capital, and to permission for Europeans to trade in the interior of China, they would lose their heads. But the British ambassador met the point by arguing that an exhibition of allied force would give the mandarins some cover for their action, and the treaty was signed on the evening of Saturday, 26 June.[2] Whatever the delays imposed from without, no one could doubt the rapidity of Elgin's action when his hands were freed. On 5 July he was able to send home a letter and copy of an imperial decree containing the Emperor's assent.[3] On 6 July he asked the admiral to afford him

---

[1] Oliphant, *Lord Elgin's Mission to China and Japan* (Harper, 1860), pp. 234-5.

[2] Letters to Lady Elgin, 29 June, 1858.

[3] Elgin to Malmesbury, 5 July, 1858.

a respectable naval force to convey him to Japan. On 8 July he had left for Shanghai, and his brother, who was ultimately to take over ambassadorial duties at Peking, and whom he counted his right arm, sailed for home with the treaty. Nothing now remained except to rectify the situation which still remained obscure at Canton, and to await the arrival of the Chinese commissioners, who were to arrange a revised tariff with the English mission at Shanghai. After speeding up movements at Peking by the threat of another visit to Tientsin, and receiving a promise that Kweiliang and Hwashana would soon arrive at Shanghai, Lord Elgin set off, post haste, on what was to prove the most charming and romantic, and by no means the least useful part of his mission, a visit to Japan. " I am off to-morrow morning for Nagasaki," he wrote home on 30 July.

There were those, like Parkes, who thought that the treaty should have been dictated at Peking, instead of being negotiated at Tientsin. But in the first place it was not certain that the highest authorities would have awaited the coming of the barbarians. It is not certain that there was an allied force adequate to take and hold the capital ; and it is clear that a little more discredit might have overthrown the central government altogether without affording a particle of help to the

SIGNING OF TREATY BETWEEN GREAT BRITAIN AND CHINA AT TIENTSIN, 26 JUNE, 1858.

From a Water-colour Drawing by F. le B Bedwell.

Western powers. As things stood in June, 1858, it was unlikely that a treaty bearing the name of Peking would have been one whit more authoritative than that which led to trouble in 1859 ; and Elgin could at least claim that his moderation had probably saved the heads of the two amiable mandarins with whom he had dealt. Signed in 1858, and reconfirmed in 1860, the Treaty of Tientsin marks the second great step forward in English trade relations with the Chinese empire. The official report to Lord Malmesbury best describes Lord Elgin's objects and his achievements :

" I have the honour to transmit herewith a Treaty signed on 26 June, 1858, by me, on behalf of Her Majesty the Queen of Great Britain, and by the Imperial Commissioners Kweiliang and Hwashana, on behalf of His Majesty the Emperor of China.

" The concessions obtained in it from the Chinese government are not in themselves extravagant ; nor, with the exception of the important principle of exterritoriality, in excess of those which commercial nations are wont freely to grant to each other ; but, in the eyes of the Chinese government, they amount to a revolution, and involve the surrender of some of the most cherished principles of the traditional policy of the empire. They have been extorted, therefore, from its fears.

" These concessions, moreover, thus extorted from the fears of the Chinese government by British and French power, are not, in point of fact, extorted from it for the benefit of British and French subjects exclusively. Under the guarantee of most favoured nation clauses, and other pretences not always so intelligible, they will no doubt be claimed and exercised very generally by the subjects and citizens of other Occidental nations. . . .

" In framing the clauses of the Treaty herewith submitted, I have been not unmindful of the claims which, on these grounds, the Chinese government has on our forbearance and moderation. Morality apart, it is not for our interest that concessions extorted from the Chinese government by British arms, should be employed by British subjects or others for the promotion of rebellion and disorder within the empire, or for the establishment of privileged smuggling and piracy along its coast and up its rivers.

" The principal commercial advantages conceded to British subjects by the Chinese government in this Treaty, are the opening to trade of certain ports, among which I would specify that of Newchwang in the north, and those which are opened by it in the Yang-tze river, Formosa, and Hainan, as the most important ; permission to British subjects to travel in the country for purposes of trade, under a system of passports ; and the settlement of the vexed question of the transit duties.

" This last mentioned subject presented considerable difficulty. As duties of octroi are levied universally in China, on native as well as foreign products, and as canals and roads are kept up at the expense of the government, it seemed to be unreasonable to require that articles, whether of foreign or native production, by the simple process of passing into the hands of foreigners, should become entitled to the use of roads and canals toll-free ; and should, moreover, be relieved altogether from charges to which they would be liable if the property of natives.

" On the other hand, experience had taught us the

inconvenience of leaving the amount of duties payable under the head of transit-duties altogether undetermined. By requiring the rates of transit-duty to be published at each port, and by acquiring for the British subject the right to commute the said duties for a payment of $2\frac{1}{2}$ per cent on the value of his goods (or rather, to speak more correctly, for the payment of a specific duty calculated at that rate), I hope that I have provided for the latter as effectual a guarantee against undue exactions on this head as can be obtained without an entire subversion of the financial system of China.

" Article VIII provides for the security of persons professing or teaching the Christian religion. The Chinese government is not bigoted in matters of religion, and any objection which it entertains to this article arises, I believe, wholly from the apprehension that it may be abused for political purposes. Time will show whether or not their apprehensions are well founded.

" But the concession in this Treaty which is, I believe, pregnant with the most important consequences to China, is that of the principle that a British minister may henceforward reside at Pekin, and hold direct intercourse with the Imperial ministers at the capital. I am confident that so long as the system of entrusting the conduct of foreign affairs to a Provincial government endures, there can be no security for the maintenance of pacific relations with this country.

" In the first place, a Provincial Governor in China cares for nothing but the interests of his own province. He regards those of other provinces of the empire rather as a jealous rival than as a protector. Nowhere in China, except at Pekin, does any solicitude for the general interests of the empire, any sentiment which answers to our idea of nationality, exist, even in pretension. A

Provincial Governor, therefore, charged with the conduct of the affairs of foreign nations who have general treaties with China, is in a false position from the outset ; and even if he were empowered to exercise an independent judgment on the questions that arise for consideration and decision, he could hardly be expected to look at them from a true point of view.

" But, in the next place, even if this preliminary difficulty were overcome, and if a Provincial Governor charged with the conduct of foreign affairs were to recognize the importance of administering them in a large and liberal spirit, it is manifest that he is not in a position to exercise in such matters an independent judgment. His life and fortune are absolutely at the disposal of a jealous government, which is, in respect to all questions of foreign policy, profoundly ignorant, and which must continue to be so, so long as the Department for Foreign Affairs is established in the provinces. In nine cases out of ten he risks both, if he even ventures to bring to the knowledge of his Sovereign an unwelcome truth.

" When a case of difficulty arises, as in a recent instance at Canton, ruin stares him in the face, with almost equal certainty, whether he resists or yields. In ordinary circumstances, his most prudent course, and therefore the one generally followed, is to allow abuses to pass unnoticed rather than incur the danger of getting into difficulties with foreigners.

" In my despatches, I called the Earl of Clarendon's attention to certain facts illustrative of the inconveniences to which this state of matters gives rise, that fell under my own notice on my visit to the different open ports. A culpable laxity, whereby the worst class of foreigners profit at the cost of the more respectable, alternating with a stolid resistance to the most reasonable proposals, leading to complications which can be disentangled only by the sword, is, in sum, the result of the working of the present system. I believe that a discreet and just representative of Great Britain, in direct communication with the officers of the Imperial Government at the capital and ready to give them advice when required, would be able to do much to cut off the source of these dangers and scandals ; and that by proving to the Imperial Government that we have no sinister designs against the empire, and no desire to protect from due punishment British subjects or others who misconduct themselves, he would mitigate the prejudices against foreigners which now influence the Imperial Councils, and which are the offspring, at least as much of fear as of pride.

" It is provided that the ratifications of this Treaty shall be exchanged at Pekin within a year from the date of its signature."[1]

It will be remembered that a mission to Japan was indicated in Lord Elgin's instructions as a proper sequel to his work in China.

" I do not think it necessary to give your Excellency any detailed instructions for your negotiations with the Japanese government," Clarendon had said. " The object to be kept in view by Your Excellency is to establish commercial relations with Japan upon at least as favourable a footing as that on which they will be placed in China. We desire no exclusive advantage for British trade ; but on the contrary are anxious that other countries should reap the full benefit of our exertions for the promotion of civilization and commerce."[2]

---

[1] Elgin to Malmesbury, 12 July, 1858.
[2] Clarendon to Elgin, 20 April, 1857.

He further added that the government did not desire to impose a new treaty on Japan by forcible means. But when the ambassador determined to utilize the interval before the Chinese envoys should arrive at Shanghai in visiting Japan, there seemed little chance of any permanent results. Japan had kept herself even more jealousy to herself than China : and apart from his general instructions, Elgin had no formal credentials to the head of the Japanese state. In China he had had the highly expert services of Wade, Parkes and Lay, but now he was launching off on a voyage of discovery without any interpreter, and, in Japan, Dutch was the only easy medium of communication with foreigners. With troubles thus offering themselves on all hands, and with something like the certainty of delays, there was no time for anything but the smoothest and rapidest of negotiations. The amazing thing was that by 26 August, he had signed a treaty which, in importance for the future, was comparable to that which had been made with China fourteen weary months after the mission had started.

The Japanese adventure was indeed a kind of oasis in the desert of Chinese troubles, and the month spent on it was certainly the happiest for Elgin between March, 1857, and his return in 1859 to England. He was at the very top of his diplomatic form, and missed not one opportunity for assisting the credit and advantage of England in Japan. The setting of Japanese scenery pleased and soothed the whole mission : " I have seen nothing so beautiful in point of scenery for many a long day," he wrote from Nagasaki on the arrival in Japan.[1] He was no longer conscious of an undercurrent of European stupidity or brutality, and from first to last, in spite of language difficulties, liked, and succeeded in the friendliest dealings with, his hosts. There was a note of audacity— almost to the point of recklessness—in his procedure. He saw that nothing would happen if he remained at Nagasaki, and so he pushed on towards Yeddo. At Simoda he found a useful friend in Harris, the Consul-General of the United States, who had just arrived, fresh from the making of a new treaty at the capital ; and interpreting difficulties vanished when the American minister lent him " the service of his own secretary and interpreter, a Dutch gentleman by name Heuskin." The British Government intended to present a yacht to the " Japanese Emperor," and with happy effrontery Lord Elgin meant this gift to act as the means of introduction to the Japanese government, and secure his entrance within the regular barriers which shut Japan off from the outer world. Find-

[1] Letters to Lady Elgin, 3 August, 1858.

ing the port at Kanagawa, ordinarily the limit prescribed to outsiders, too far off to serve his purposes, he pushed on to within five miles of the capital, and thence he secured both the freest permission to land and all the commercial concessions he desired. It was a time of mutual feasts, excursions round the environs of Yeddo, and extravagant purchases of Japanese commodities which ranged from lacquered articles to Japanese dogs. The American treaty of 20 July, had given a model on which to base his requests, and he found the statesmen with whom he had to deal everything that the Chinese mandarins were not. To the home government he praised the intelligence and amiability of the people with whom he had to deal ; in his home letters he called them " a most curious contrast to the Chinese, so anxious to learn and so *prevenants*." On 18 August, he placed in the hands of the Japanese commissioners a draft treaty, written in Dutch, and exactly one month from the signing of the treaty of Tientsin, he concluded what, with that document, was to form the foundation of British trade in the Far East. The visit concluded with a very characteristic exhibition of his amiable and profitable guile.

" The Japanese authorities," he wrote to Malmesbury, " have never hitherto, either at Nagasaki or elsewhere, been brought to consent to salute a foreign flag. I thought the occasion a favourable one for inducing them to break through their practice in this particular. I proposed, therefore, to the ministers, that the yacht should be handed over to the Japanese government on the day of the signature of the Treaty ; that the British flag should, in the first place, be hoisted at the main, and saluted with twenty-one guns by the Japanese forts ; that the Japanese flag should then be substituted for it, and saluted by the British ships. At their request I put this proposal in writing. It was agreed to, after due deliberation, and the result was that on the 26th instant, at the hour appointed, the British flag was saluted from the forts of Yeddo with twenty-one guns of large calibre, fired with an accuracy and good effect which, in my experience of salutes, I have never heard surpassed."

A brilliant illumination of the Yeddo forts closed the episode, and the mission departed, surfeited with novel experiences, and bearing with them a treaty which gave Great Britain all that could reasonably be expected, including the power to appoint a diplomatic agent at Yeddo, exterritorial rights, permission to British subjects to buy and sell directly ; and a reduction of export duties from 35 per cent to a general rate of 5 per cent *ad valorem*. Well might Laurence Oliphant, who obviously enjoyed every moment of his stay in Japan, declare that the experiences of the mission had been marked by an interest and a novelty not to be surpassed, and by a success, in a political point of view, scarcely to have been anticipated.[1]

With the return to Shanghai, on 2 September, the region of probable storms was once more reached. In comparison with the novelty and fairyland atmosphere of Japan, Shanghai seemed a very dull place inhabited by European residents engaged in making vast fortunes and being bored in the process.[2] But the serious problem came from Peking not Shanghai. The tariff commissioners lingered on the road, and their pace had to be quickened by a reminder that the season was not too far advanced for another visit to Tientsin. Even after his old friends Kweiliang and Hwashana appeared early in October, Elgin found that he had once more to resort to diplomatic conflict. Things had been going none too well at Canton. Braves were being enlisted for offensive purposes ; incidents which involved bloodshed were occurring, and a new bribe of 30,000 dollars was publicly offered for Harry Parkes' head. Elgin at once refused to begin business until these matters were put right, and he told the commissioners firmly that no measure would be acceptable which fell short of removing Yeh's successor from his

[1] Authorities : China Corr. II, pp. 366–382 ; Letters to Lady Elgin, 3 August–27 August ; Oliphant, *op. cit.*
[2] Letters to Lady Elgin, 9 September, 1858.

Governorship, and withdrawing from the Kwantung gentry the special military powers with which they were invested.

The tariff revision which had been placed in the hands of Oliphant and Wade belongs rather to the economic history of the European communities in China than to the biography of Lord Elgin, but the ambassador felt himself impelled to take special notice of the opium trade. He had never acquiesced in the impossible situation at the ports where a trade prohibited by Chinese law was carried briskly on by Westerners, especially Americans and Englishmen. Chinese legal demands were indeed exacting, but the system of prohibition was a pure farce, so merchants grew rich, China reaped an illicit revenue, and smuggling with all its companion blackguardries flourished everywhere. After a correspondence with the American minister Reed, which did great credit to the sense of justice as well as to the shrewdness of both men, Elgin found a suitable formula : " I have little doubt," he wrote, " but that it will be found that legislation is the only available remedy."[1] It has always seemed better to British statesmen, and, in 1858, also to the representative of the United States, that moderate restrictive laws should be obeyed than that absolute legal prohibition should be

[1] China Corr. II, pp. 393–400.

accepted, and stultified by acquiescence in lawless-
ness. So, after much discussion, it was agreed
that 30 taels per chest should be the duty levied,
and that both Treaty powers and Chinese should
co-operate in securing obedience to the law.

There was another vexed question, the compromising solution of which called down on the
plenipotentiary's head the criticisms of his Anglo-
Chinese critics. But here Lord Elgin must state his
own case. The arrangements had been practically
completed, and Elgin was anxious, although formally he had no legal rights until the Treaty of
Tientsin was ratified, to sail up the Yangtze river as
far as the great trade centre Hankow ; but meantime he found his Chinese colleagues in a quandary.
Peking was seriously distressed over the proposed
residence of foreign representatives. As Kweiliang
and Hwashana pointed out :

" If we were quite sure that you would always send us
men thoroughly wise, discreet and considerate, it might
be different, but if, for instance, So-and-so were appointed
to represent a foreign government at Pekin—a month
would not elapse before something would occur which
would place our highest officers in the dilemma of having
either to risk a quarrel or submit to some indignity which
would lower the Chinese government in the eyes of its
own subjects."

There was the inter-connected question of
rebuilding the Peiho forts, and the reorganization

of the outer defences of the capital. If the commissioners, for whom Elgin had now a not unkindly feeling, were to report complete failure to modify the extreme rigour of the treaty, he feared that their degradation and punishment would be inevitable.

" The upshot of it all is this," he reported, " that after reserving, in the most unqualified terms, Her Majesty's right to exercise as she may see fit the option conferred on Her by Article III of the Treaty of Tientsin, I have undertaken to communicate with H.M.'s Government the representations which have been made to me on the subject by the Chinese Imperial Commissioners, and humbly to submit it as my opinion that if H.M.'s ambassador be properly received at Pekin, when the ratifications are exchanged next year, and full effect given in all other particulars to the Treaty—it will be expedient that H.M.'s representative in China be instructed to choose a place of residence elsewhere than at Pekin, and to make his visits to the capital either periodically, or as frequently as the exigencies of the public service may require."[1]

Advocates of the strong hand, when events gave them their opening in 1859, blamed Elgin, firstly for his failure to push on to Peking, and secondly for his concession on this point. All that need be said here is that it was Elgin's decency and moderation which took from the whole negotiation the suggestion of mere force which otherwise it would have presented ; and that, whatever he might have done

[1] Elgin to Malmesbury, 5 November, 1858.

239

or left undone, it is most probable that the tragedy of the Taku forts would still have been enacted in 1859. As it was, not only did the American minister, as is obvious from all his letters, carry away a sense of English justice and moderation, but the two Chinese commissioners, in one of their latest communications, praised with an obvious sincerity His Excellency's " friendly dispositions and forethoughtful care."[1]

The long story of the first mission is now nearly at an end. But before their departure, the much enduring diplomatists ventured on their second romantic voyage, a 600-mile sail up the Yangtze to Hankow. It is unnecessary to rehearse what Laurence Oliphant has dealt with so charmingly in his narrative ; how the *Repulse* and her sister ships passed " into an unknown region, along a river which, beyond Nanking, had not been navigated by Europeans ; " how they explored, and grounded, and overcame the difficulties of navigation ; how they subdued the Tai-ping rebels at Nanking, penetrated to Hankow, forced the authorities of those regions to recognize them, and found that the fall of the river almost prevented their return in December. It was a holiday for all concerned, even when it came to temporary

[1] Kweiliang and Hwashana to Lord Elgin, 17 January, 1859.

hostilities with the Tai-pings, and it was not unnatural for a devoted Scot like Elgin, to compare,
now this, now that glimpse of Chinese scenery
to Loch Katrine, or Ardgowan, or the Highlands.
They found the people desirous to buy and sell ;
and it was clear that if only the authorities were
firmly and tactfully dealt with, all would go well.
So the argonauts came and went, leaving Shanghai
on 8 November, and returning thither on New
Year's afternoon, 1859.[1] Little more remained to
be done. The Shanghai merchants received some
good advice from the ambassador before the
mission passed South. From Hong-Kong and
Canton, where military action was still necessary
to quell the turbulence of the country braves, Elgin
once more warned the Peking government that
their authority must be asserted on the side of peace.
Arrangements were made for a force of gunboats
to escort Frederick Bruce when he returned to
complete at Peking the ratification of the treaties.
Then at last the tired ambassador was able to
enter in his journal for 3 March, 1859, the cheering
words : " I am really and truly off on·my way to
England, though I can hardly believe that it is so."
One further duty connected with the mission

[1] For this adventure see Oliphant, pp. 491–598 ; Letters
to Lady Elgin, pp. 131–162 ; China Corr. II, pp. 440–452,
with map.

still remained—the interchange with his brother Frederick, at Ceylon, of views on China which might simplify the performance of his new important functions at Peking. Then, on 19 May, Lord Elgin " had the honour to apprize " the Foreign Secretary that he had returned from his mission, after relieving India, capturing Canton, almost attaining Peking, exploring Japan and the Yangtze river, and concluding two fundamentally important treaties with the two greatest of Asiatic powers.

Enough of comment has been passed already on the spirit in which Lord Elgin had approached his painfully responsible tasks. The chapter may fitly end with a paragraph from his reply to the Shanghai merchants which expressed not only his own views, but something of the ideals which have helped to save the empire which he served from mere political materialism :

" Uninvited, and by methods not always of the gentlest, we have broken down the barriers behind which these ancient nations sought to conceal from the world without the mysteries, perhaps also in the case of China at least, the rags and rottenness of their waning civilizations. Neither our own consciences nor the judgment of mankind will acquit us if, when we are asked to what use we have turned our opportunities, we can only say that we have filled our pockets from among the ruins which we have found or made."[1]

[1] China Corr. II, p. 458.

CHAPTER VI

THE SECOND MISSION TO CHINA,
1860-61

THE second halting place in Lord Elgin's
service overseas occurred on his return
from China ; from the middle of May,
1859, to the end of April, 1860, it almost seemed
as though home politics were to claim him and
convert him into a cabinet minister. The Chinese
mission, possessing a higher spectacular value
than the Canadian Governorship, had brought
him prominently before men's eyes, and prepared
the way for Palmerston's offer of the position of
Postmaster-General in the Whig ministry of 1859.[1]
There he met, not only old Peelite friends like
Herbert and Gladstone, but the Whigs who had
so faithfully supported him through his Canadian
difficulties. The clearest view of him as a cabinet
minister may be gathered from the very intimate
letters which, throughout those years, Earl Gran-

[1] June, 1859.

243

ville was writing to his friend Canning in India.[1]
It is plain that Granville and Elgin were very
different men, and that one need not look for
entire sympathy in Granville's comments on his
colleague. Yet the general impression conveyed
is not unjust. Granville thought that the Post-
mastership was a disappointment. He also noted
Elgin's silence and reserve in cabinet meetings.[2]
The truth was that in a cabinet whose two chief
men, Palmerston and Russell, were both European
nationalists, there was one dominating interest,
Italy and her relations with France and Austria ;
and Elgin's career had led him far away from
continental diplomacy. He took part several times
in the spring of 1860 in debates on China ; but it
would be absurd to regard him as a leader in a
ministry rendered illustrious by Gladstone's finance,
and Russell's and Palmerston's defence of Italian
unity.

The autumn of 1859 had been spent in Scotland,
including ten days as cabinet minister at Balmoral.
Various public functions called for his presence ;
and before the second summons to China came,
he had scored an innocent political victory by

[1] Palmerston had given Granville permission to write freely
to Canning, even of cabinet secrets.

[2] Fitzmaurice, *Life of Lord Granville* : correspondence with
Canning during 1859 and 1860.

EXCHANGE OF POWERS BETWEEN GREAT BRITAIN AND JAPAN, 1858.

From a Water-colour Drawing by F. le B. Bedwell.

defeating Disraeli for the Rectorship of Glasgow University, where he counted 553 votes to Disraeli's 411. More interesting even than the oration which he delivered to his young constituents were the comments which his election drew from the journals of the day. *The Morning Herald* spoke of him as " one of the regular Whig team ; " and *The Glasgow Herald* in explaining Disraeli's defeat thought that " doubtless his (Elgin's) political creed stood him in good stead in a community which goes a long way in the Liberal direction." [1] It is clear that, as with Gladstone and other Peelites, the country thought of him in 1859 as one of the coming Liberal Party.

But unexpected events in China cut short the period of Lord Elgin's one adventure in British Cabinet Government.

On 25 June, 1859, the British admiral, whose duty it was to convey Frederick Bruce up the Peiho river, on his way to exchange the ratifications of the Treaty of Tientsin at Peking, was attacked as he endeavoured to clear away the obstructions at the river mouth, and he was compelled to withdraw his forces after suffering heavy losses. With that event Lord Elgin, although for the moment it did not seem to affect more than his

[1] *The Glasgow Herald*, 16 November, and 19 November, 1859.

prestige as ambassador, entered on another chapter of his adventures. His second mission to China was a direct sequel to his first, and although, as always happens with sequels, he entered on it with some reluctance, events gave the campaign which followed an interest and sensational importance which were lacking in the slow and gradual processes of the first.

The misfortune to Admiral Hope and Frederick Bruce's mission, was the natural occasion for adverse comments on the settlement at Tientsin, and the methods by which it had been settled. It is only too easy for a biographer to adopt the attitude either of unsympathetic critic, or of earnest apologist. The truth is better served by a cool appreciation of the state of affairs then existing in China.

The Treaty of Tientsin had been made with an empire, inorganic or at best invertebrate. At Peking there existed a government, completely autocratic in intention, and formally accepted with religious reverence throughout such of the provinces as were not in the hands of rebels. But outside Peking, and more especially in relations with the Western powers, the most extraordinary laxity and latitude were conceded to provincial authorities ; so that the official attitude of the Chinese empire towards the diplomatic and

246

domestic problems which it faced varied with local circumstances, and the temper of individual Gover- nors. In 1858 there had been war with the Western powers at Canton ; diplomatic rigour on the Peiho ; perfect peace at Shanghai ; and Imperial Commissioners spoke to the Western plenipoten- tiaries in the accents of friendship while an allied force was holding Canton by the strong hand. In the same way the insensitive government at Peking diminished not one iota of its dignity and hauteur although on the Yangtze Nanking had long been the capital of a tremendous rebellion, which had once threatened the capital, and which in 1859 was advancing to attack the ports at the river mouth. The empire was indeed a vast, ill-con- nected body in which peace and war, disorder and strict autocracy, might co-exist without any acute sense of discomfort at the centre. It was not a *state* in the sense in which that term is com- monly used in the West. Its Emperor was a figure- head, moved to suit the purposes of peace faction or war faction, as each obtained control of the central authority ; and, whatever rule prevailed, there was no feeling of obligation, especially towards " barbarians," to be bound by agreements made by a preceding ministry, or a local representative. Possessed by a blinding sense of the impregnable sanctity of Imperial authority, whatever power held sway at Peking claimed the right to act without reference to previous engagements, or political reason, or the claims of mere fact. Elgin had spoken to Clarendon of " the inconsistency which characterizes everything in China ; "[1] he might have used a stronger term. It was the result of a decline in the potency of the ruling dynasty operating in an ultra-oriental fabric of government, and exaggerated by the extent of the territory and the numbers of the population concerned.

The other side of this political abnormality was the complete indifference, except under very special orders, of the various provincial populations to anything but their own national, useful, industrious pursuits. An acute observer had pointed out to a previous British minister, " the utter indifference of the people as to what dynasty or power is dominant so long as they are allowed to raise their rice in peace, and their own immediate fields are not made the scene of the struggle."[2] Both in 1858 and 1860 the British mission noted that even on the Peiho, on the highway to the capital, the country folk accepted the advance of the invaders as an ordinary and almost friendly phenomenon. There was something even admirable in the resolute refusal of the ordinary population to be

[1] 2 April, 1858.
[2] Mitchell to Bonham, 15 March, 1852.

248

bullied into resistance or outrage, and the rightful practice of pacificism has never been better illustrated than in a case which Elgin quoted from Talienwan where the British army had gathered in 1860.

" A few days ago, a party of drunken sailors went to a village, got into a row, and killed a man by mistake. On the day following, three officers went to the village armed with revolvers. The villagers surrounded them, took from them the revolvers (whether the officers fired or not is disputed) and then conducted them, without doing them any injury, to their boat. An officer, with an interpreter, was then sent to the village to ask for the revolvers. They were at once given up, the villagers stating that they had no wish to take them, but that as one of their number had been shot already, they *objected to people coming to them with arms.*"[1]

In its relations, political, commercial, and religious, with this strange world, European civilization brought against their Chinese hosts the charges of treachery and bad faith, and indeed the Western-minded historian need not look outside the years 1857–60 for glaring examples of these sins. But once more it is necessary to appreciate the Chinese point of view. Barbarians " uncontrollably fierce " had come to thrust on them, no doubt to their advantage, Western trade ; religious opinions, of an unintelligible description, were being pro-

[1] Letters to Lady Elgin, 9 July, 1860.

claimed,[1] sometimes under the protection of Western official threats ; their political seclusion which they dearly cherished was being rudely broken into. To support these invasions, the foreign governments were exacting by force a series of written agreements ; but as the things protected did not, either to government or to people, seem other than violent greed, dangerous propaganda, and unwarrantably bad manners, they counted it a light thing to match these evils with cunning, and a refusal to abide by promises extorted from them. Nowhere did Lord Elgin show more of that unromantic insight and sense of proportion which so distinguished him, than when, after the unpardonable outrage on his diplomatic agents and their escort, which will be related below, he did not accuse his opponents of carefully prepared treachery :

" To hazard conjectures as to the motives by which Chinese functionaries are actuated is not a very safe undertaking ; and it is very possible that further information may modify the view which I now entertain on this point. I am, however, disposed at present to doubt there having been a deliberate intention of treachery—I apprehend that the general-in-chief thought that he (the Chinese commissioner) had compromised his military position by allowing our army to establish itself so near

[1] The Tai-ping manifestos, with their fantastic perversions of Christian myth, illustrate well this unintelligibility.

his lines at Chang-kia-wan. He sought to counteract the evil effect of this by making a great swagger of parade and preparation to resist when the allied armies approached the camping ground allotted to them."[1]

It is necessary to insist on the fact that between 1842 and 1861 two civilizations so different in temper, traditions, and principles, were being brought into unexpected contact by Western trade and by the political protection of that trade ; and that the time of contact was one when it would have been easy to shake the whole organization, such as it was, of China into ruin. To men of the type of Harry Parkes, although Parkes was infinitely wiser, more modest and more reflective than the ordinary " empire-builder," it seemed that resolute aggression, and a refusal to compromise was the only possible attitude. It might have been, if England, France and Russia had been prepared to reproduce in China between 1857 and 1861 situations such as Clive and Dupleix had once faced in India, or Europe was still fretting herself over in Turkey. But neither the British public, with its half-honest muddle-pated views, nor European diplomacy, which had too many vexed questions already on hand, nor Palmerston, who even in Turkey disliked schemes of partition, would consent to hastening a general Chinese

[1] Elgin to Russell, 23 September, 1860.

cataclysm. Elgin, who knew, as his Anglo-Chinese critics never even tried to know, the limits prescribed in Europe to his action, and who, in his own enlightened conscience, had an entire distrust of forcible logic, had to shape things as best he could on principles of honesty, mercy and justice. It was no wonder that he had taken long to reconcile the Chinese to the concession of treaty privileges ; or that he had to reconstruct in 1860 what he had thought secure in 1858. Under whatever conditions the Tientsin agreement might have been made and at whatever place, even Peking, there was still no guarantee except that of a large and permanently established garrison in North China, that the conditions would be maintained by the Chinese one minute longer than their weakness forced them to yield. That garrison, and the diplomatic consequences flowing from its maintenance, would have precipitated troubles in Europe, incomparably more harassing than those of the near East had ever been. Diplomatic progress, especially at its most decisive moments, moves by inches, and in curves, except for the arm-chair statesman and the would-be Napoleon.

Since this was the condition of affairs in China, it was not wonderful that the affair of the Taku forts occurred when it did ; and to mend the situation no one better fitted to set things right could have been chosen than the negotiator of the insulted treaty. But before he left England on 26 April, 1860, two decisive steps had been taken. Frederick Bruce had despatched an ultimatum to the senior Secretary of State at Peking, demanding an apology for the outrage, the completion of the treaty ratification, provision for the entrance of himself and his suite into Peking, and the payment of the indemnity stipulated for in the treaty.[1] Before this had been despatched the British Government had arranged with their French allies, for a joint force, 10,000 strong from Great Britain, 8,000 from France, with adequate naval support, to be concentrated in the North of China, Sidney Herbert at the War Office prescribing to the British Commander-in-Chief, Sir Hope Grant, that hostilities should be confined to that part of the Chinese empire in which the outrage had been committed.[2] What the attitude of the war party now in control at Peking was likely to be might be gathered from an Imperial decree which had bestowed posthumous honours on those who fell at Taku and rejoicing " that the rebellious English had received a lesson which will deter them

[1] China Corr. III, pp. 34–36.
[2] S. Herbert to Sir Hope Grant, 9 January, 1860. The numbers of the two forces given above are only those of the preliminary estimates. The force actually employed was stronger.

from again provoking the martial dignity of the Celestial empire."[1]

The instructions with which Lord Elgin left London were partly explicit, partly suggestions to be developed into practice according as circumstances dictated in China. The three indispensable conditions have already been described—apology, ratification and indemnity. The expedition was a joint one with France, and Lord John Russell thought it essential that the ambassadors should be received at Peking with honour. But the obvious danger that in the course of the campaign the Chinese government might suffer fatal ruin, and reflection on the possible consequences of such a catastrophe forced the government to leave ultimate decisions as completely in the hands of the plenipotentiaries as in the previous mission. Continual reference to French co-operation would prove distracting in the following narrative, so it may be well here to record one or two facts concerning it. The quarrel, as in 1856, was almost wholly a British one, but France was conscious, not to say jealous, of the assertion of British rights in China, and co-operation was the price paid by Britain for that very doubtful benefit, her alliance with Napoleon III. With Baron Gros Elgin maintained the friendliest of relations, but

[1] F. Bruce to Admiral Hope, 6 January, 1860.

it may be doubted whether General de Montauban, to be renamed later the Comte de Palikao from one of the easy victories of this campaign, was specially welcome or useful to his admirable Anglo-Indian colleague, Hope Grant. The second Napoleonic empire, already overburdened with projects, could not lavish so much expense as its ally did, on preparations. The French contingent undoubtedly delayed the start of operations by its deficiencies. On a major point of strategy, at the start, Hope Grant had to force his opinion on an unwilling French colleague, and there can be no doubt that at Chusan, at the mouth of the Peiho, and more especially in the Summer Palace at Peking, the French troops brought shame on their country and European civilization by unrestrained plunder and destruction. The utmost that can be said for them on this last point is that Garnet Wolseley who watched officers and men " seized with a temporary insanity ; in body and soul absorbed in one pursuit, plunder, plunder," believed that looting was not " attended with such demoralizing effect in the French army as it was in ours."[1] It seems probable that the convention which ended the affair might have been signed a month earlier than it was, had Hope Grant had sole control of operations.

[1] Wolseley, *Narrative of the China War*, p. 227.

Lord Elgin left Britain in a mood much more subdued than can be detected in any of his other enterprises. He confessed to Lady Elgin that he wrote his journal " with a more leaden pen than formerly." He seemed to be ordered out to correct faults of which he was in part author, and there was little credit to be gained from work of mere rectification. He was displacing, for the time, his brother Frederick. It was a difficult and unwelcome errand, and it would be no counterbalancing advantage if he were to find, on arriving in China, that a settlement had been arrived at, and that all his travelling had been for nothing. Nor was there now the novelty which had made the wanderings of the first mission a real voyage of discovery. At Point de Galle, which he reached towards the end of May, despondency was relieved by the shock of a shipwreck ; for the *Malabar*, on which he was to sail to China, was caught in a violent change of wind just before starting, and had to be grounded in deep water by her captain. Two glimpses of the ambassador in affliction are memorable—in one, his approach, urged by the anxieties of the passengers, to ask if the captain really meant to put to sea. " Going to sea," said the captain with the cheerful pessimism of an expert, " why, we are going to the bottom."[1] The other is Loch's

[1] Letters to Lady Elgin, 23 May, 1860.

picture of Elgin and Gros quietly seated on the poop of the *Malabar* in the height of the crisis, " conversing together as if no danger impended."[1] Happily he was able to record, day by day, the recovery of his property—first some cases of champagne (the Western article of diplomatic exchange for Chinese tea) and a box of linen ; then his decorations, sea-soiled but not entirely ruined ; then his full powers, happily still legible. His letter of credence was lost.

In this fashion he entered the Eastern seas. By 21 June he arrived at Hong-Kong, and from that point onwards, subject only to the delays of the French, and the procrastinating diplomacy of the Chinese, he pressed on until the final settlement was reached. His first duty was to define with his French colleague the preliminary attitude of the allied missions towards Peking. They were in a dilemma. The ultimatum had been rejected, but no act of hostility had accompanied or followed the rejection. If they intimated their arrival to the Chinese government, without armed pressure, they would be at once involved in intricate and useless discussions, or, if they cut these short, they might find themselves seemingly rejecting reasonable terms. In a memorandum to Gros, Elgin anchored himself on the ultimatum, and proposed

[1] Loch, *Personal Narrative*, p. 13.

that he and Gros should conform their conduct to the movements of the soldiers, following closely behind these in readiness to receive whatever overtures the Chinese government might make. His purpose was, if possible, to address his first note to Peking from Tientsin.[1] At Hong-Kong he invited into the mission, the other chief hero of the expedition, Harry Parkes. Parkes, and if one may believe his biographer, others of the interpreting staff, had not been taken into Lord Elgin's confidence in the earlier affair.[2] The truth was that the ambassador had found the " vigorous policy " party so strong in China, he had observed so many exhibitions of inhumanity of temper towards the Chinese, and he had disapproved so entirely of the methods of levying private war followed by Bowring, Seymour, and Parkes over the *Arrow*, that he could hardly have been expected to take the Anglo-Chinese leaders unreservedly into his confidence. On the other hand, Parkes, whose dealings with his chief had been confined to the Canton episode, did not know his man, and, with that passionate devotion to British interests in China, and that unique knowledge of local politics which so constantly made it easy to him to forget the world outside his area, he contended for no compromise, no surrender

[1] China Corr. III, pp. 87–88.
[2] Lane Poole, *Life of Sir Harry Parkes*, I, p. 339.

to Chinese wiles, and free access to Peking forced
at the points of British bayonets. He was not in-
humane—rather the contrary; and his was undoubtedly the plan in outline which his chief would
have to take and modify to suit the general policy
of Great Britain; but it was well for both sides
that they were now flung together, and learned
how useful each could be to the other. When all
was about to end, and Lord Elgin, to use Parkes'
words, " evinced some feeling in bidding me good-
bye," the famous consul confessed that the event
did not add to his good spirits and that he went
ashore feeling a little downcast.[1] The great man
had proved less of a sinophil Jupiter than he had
thought. How deeply impressed the chief was
with his assistant the journal to Lady Elgin testifies :
" Parkes is one of the most remarkable men I ever
met," he wrote ; " for energy, courage and ability
combined I do not know where I could find his
match ; and this, joined to a faculty of speaking
Chinese which he shares only with Lay, makes him
at present *the* man of the situation."[2] In the whole
adventure Parkes was ubiquitous, essential, and
untiring ; and he earned for himself the distinction
of being counted by the highest Chinese authorities
as influential as the ministers themselves. For,

[1] Lane Poole, *Life of Sir Harry Parkes*, I, p. 407.
[2] Letters to Lady Elgin, 14 September, 1860.

when captive, he was assailed by the Chinese Commander-in-Chief himself with demands for the reversal of the allied plans : " You say that you do not direct these military movements," said Sangkolinsin to his prisoner, " but I know your name and that you instigate all the evils that your people commit."[1] Both Elgin and Parkes were alike in this, that they hated delay and inefficiency, and if their past experiences had differed so widely as to make common formulæ difficult, they were, in co-operation, exactly complementary, and must be counted the sole partners with the army in the final success.

Events now hurried to a definite issue. On 1 July, the ambassador was at Shanghai ; on 5 July, he had left for the North, where the allied forces were gathered—the French at Chefu, the British across the Gulf of Pechili at Talien-wan, and on 26 July he had started for the scene of action. He was greatly pleased with the British force and its commander. " Nothing," he said, " could be more perfect than the condition of the force, both men and horses " ; the quiet simplicity and kindliness of Hope Grant's manner impressed him, and he was glad to note that " there seems to be really no plundering or bullying." " When your force lands," said Ignatieff, the Russian

[1] China Corr. III, p. 330.

envoy, to him, " I give you six days to finish every-thing."[1]

The operations, however, which commenced on 31 July, by the capture of Peh-tang, a wretched town on the mud-flats north of the Peiho, did not attain their end completely until 26 October, when the definitive convention was signed at Peking. Although diplomacy and military operations waited on each other in admirable partnership, it will make for clearness if the advance on Peking be described in summary before the diplomatic strug-gle is introduced. The inspiring force on the Chinese side was Prince Sangkolinsin, whose mili-tary reputation had been gained by an earlier success against the Tai-ping rebels. Nothing either in his recorded judgments, or in his actions, betrays the first beginnings of a knowledge of the art of war. He had already declared himself satisfied that the barbarians would find it difficult to land anywhere between Taku and Peh-tang, and that if they did, his forces would repel them. " Their coming thither will amount to no more than an anchoring off it (Taku), or hanging about it, under pretence of handing in letters, to gain information on which they may have some stratagem."[2] Neglecting the prepared front at Taku, the allies easily landed their

[1] Letters to Lady Elgin, 14 July, 1860.
[2] China Corr. III, pp. 120–124.

forces a few miles north, opposed by nothing more formidable than the mud and smells of Peh-tang, and, before August was over, they were in complete control of the mouth of the Peiho, the sea-gate into Peking. To maintain pressure sufficient to give the diplomatists a chance, gunboats and army passed on to Tientsin, at which Lord Elgin himself arrived on 26 August. Then, as the battle of letters grew fierce, the army passed on by easy stages towards Tung-chow and Peking. The weight of allied strength did everything that mere diplomacy would have left unmoved, and terrified the Chinese government into sending their chief princes to try to stay the advance. At this point Sangkolinsin once more made himself felt, for after it had been settled that a position a few miles short of Tung-chow should be fixed for the allied forces while Elgin was finishing his business, the Chinese Commander-in-Chief violated the agreement which the civilians had practically completed, prepared an ambush for the unsuspecting barbarians, and laid violent hands on Parkes, Loch and a number of British and French officers and men, who had been engaged in preliminaries for the advance. This precipitated a battle. Beaten on 18 September and again on 21 September, the Chinese Commander withdrew from Peking, and indeed from history ; and the allied troops timing their actions to assist Elgin's efforts to recover the captives alive, advanced on 5 October on Peking, the main British force to the north of the city, the French and the British cavalry to the Emperor's summer palace. On 12 October a threat of bombardment delivered the Anting gate at Peking into British hands, and with Peking controlled by the allied forces one of the most completely but ingloriously successful campaigns ever fought by the British or French armies came to an end.

As for the captives, eight in all, British and French, including Parkes and Loch, were sent in on 9 October, after having received the most brutal treatment, and five days later eight troopers and one French soldier returned. But, of the British, twenty-three had perished, and of the French, at least eight. The soldiers blamed the diplomats, and especially Parkes, for the misadventure and also for almost leading them into an ambuscade; but it is difficult to see how, short of mistrusting every word and action on the Chinese side, Parkes could have acted otherwise than he did ; and the solemnity and tragedy with which the march on Peking closed, aided not a little in hastening and establishing the security of the Peking convention.

The diplomacy of the mission advanced by approximately the same stages, and culminated and modified itself at the same geographical points as did its strategy.

At first, and before Lord Elgin himself arrived, Frederick Bruce controlled negotiations. He had defined his ends clearly in the ultimatum ; at the same time he proved the merciful spirit inspiring British policy by refusing to create a commercial blockade which would have affected not the court, but the people of China. He was limited however in his operations, first by the news that an extra-ordinary mission was being sent, and secondly by the fact that the commissioners with whom he dealt were men of secondary importance—the surest proof that the Peking government did not take the negotiations seriously. Elgin's first position after he arrived was, as has been seen, to take the ultimatum as his objective, and Tientsin as the probable scene of his activities. A week after the military landing he brushed aside the advances of the Governor-General of the province, telling him that he refused to stay the march of the military forces for such manœuvres.[1] When the same official attempted to make friendly overtures from Tientsin, Elgin maintained the same stern front. His reward was the news that more important commissioners, one of them no other than his old friend Kweiliang, were on their way to Tientsin

[1] Letters to Lady Elgin, 9 August, 1860.

with full powers. These he met with the unvarying declaration " that it was not in his power
to call on the commanders-in-chief to suspend
their operations until all the demands (of the
ultimatum) had been acceded to."[1] At this point
the Chinese made their first surrender, and on
2 September Kweiliang and his colleague Hang
intimated that they were prepared to concede the
allied demands.

In response to this act of concession the ambassador now developed his position in a draft convention—substantially the text which was accepted
at Peking. The Chinese government was to apolo-
gize for its misdeeds at Taku ; to make preparations
for the entrance into Peking, England no longer
permitting the concession that the English ministers
might dwell outside the city ; the Treaty of Tientsin was to be ratified, and the new convention
accepted as if ratified ; Tientsin was to become an
open port ; indemnities were prescribed and the
Treaty and Convention were to be published in all
the provinces by Imperial decree. But it soon became apparent either that the commissioners had
not power to concede so much, or that they were at
their old game of obstruction. This move Elgin
met by an intimation that he had determined to
proceed at once to Tung-chow a few miles distant

[1] Elgin to Russell, 5 September, 1860.

from the capital, and to defer further action till that point had been reached.

This threat, reinforced by the steady progress of the armies, at once precipitated the penultimate and most startling phase of the mission. It now became plain that the Peking government, which meant, not the phantom Emperor, but the three princes who at that time dominated the council, was seriously alarmed ; for Lord Elgin now received a communication from " two of the highest functionaries of the empire, Tsai, a near relation to the Emperor, Prince of I, and Muh-yin, President of the Board of War," informing him that they were coming to Tientsin to deal with the whole matter in person.[1] To check at once the attempt at evasion, made by the new commissioners, by which the joint mission were invited to retire to Tientsin, Elgin at once replied that he adhered to his decision not to negotiate south of Tung-chow, and after some hesitation his opponents conceded almost all the points at issue unconditionally, but asked that the army might not go so far as Tung-chow—that was too near the sacred capital. Whether the slight concession made at this point had anything to do with the tragedy which followed, is a point to be answered only by those who have had practical experience of Chinese diplo-

[1] Elgin to Russell, 11 September, 1860.

266

macy ; but it is curious that the outrages on the British and French envoys of 17 and 18 September, followed shortly after Elgin's intimation " that if the Chinese authorities gave me its securities for their good conduct which I required, I would cause the army to halt at a point within an easy stage of Tung-chow, and proceed with an escort to Tung-chow, for the signature of the convention and to Peking for the exchange of the ratifications." [1]

If Elgin was deceived, and thought too optimistically of Chinese good faith (even after the event he still refused to think the treachery malice prepense), he sinned in good company, for the two greatest experts in Chinese diplomacy, Wade and Parkes, after an eight hours' interview, were so convinced of Prince Tsai's *bona fides* that their opinion in the first place persuaded the mission to march the troops to the place designated by the Imperial Commissioners, and in the second place led Parkes himself, with Henry Loch, Lord Elgin's private secretary, to involve his party in the disaster in which all of them were made captive, and most of them suffered death. Whether Sangkolinsin thought to recover all the reputation he had lost, in one wild gamble, making light of what the commissioners had promised ; or whether the whole war party, commissioners included, thought to

[1] Elgin to Russell, 16 September, 1860.

overthrow the barbarians by a surprise attack on the troops, and the possible capture of one of the " greater barbarians," it is difficult to say. At any rate, if it cost the allies a score of useful lives, it precipitated, not only the advance on Peking, but a final surrender in diplomacy. As soon as it appeared that the misguided plans of 17 and 18 September had resulted in fresh military defeats, and that Lord Elgin was not to be terrified into concession, what amounted to a *coup d'état* in the direction of Chinese affairs took place, and Prince Kung, brother to the Emperor, and reputedly the advocate at court of concession and peace, intimated that he would meet the allies, and proposed an armistice with a view to re-establish peace.[1]

The position was a painfully difficult one for Lord Elgin—in these matters his mind and no other was the deciding force. It was almost impossible to modify military operations without seriously interfering with the plans of the generals. Yet a fresh attack might mean death to all the captives. On the other hand, any sign of weakening purpose might give the war party fresh encouragement, in which case the event for the captives promised to be the same. His decision was, not to weaken in action at all, but to continue, along with military pressure, every diplomatic means at his disposal to

[1] Elgin to Russell, 23 September, 1860.

ADVANCE ON PEKING. SECOND MISSION TO CHINA, 1860.

From a Water-colour Drawing by W. Hope Crealock.

free the captives. He warned Prince Kung that until the captives were restored he could not take any steps to stay military operations ; and when Kung with that curious mixture of shrewdness and ingenuousness which the Chinese betrayed all through these years, argued that the envoys had been captured after the fight had commenced, and that they would be restored when the fleets and armies had left Taku, Elgin launched his final thunderbolt and gave three days' time for surrender, warning the Prince that the allied counterstroke would entail the destruction of Peking and the probable fall of the Manchu dynasty.[1] Strange as it may seem, even at this tragic moment when the fate of the existing dynasty seemed in the balance, Prince Kung reprimanded Elgin for the unseemliness of the threat. " The words in the despatch under acknowledgment regarding the attack on and the destruction of the capital and the downfall of the dynasty are words which indeed it is not fitting that a subject should use."[2] From 28 September until at least 4 October, this extraordinary government continued through Kung to fence with Elgin over the fate of the prisoners, and it was not until 9 October, that the chief captives, Parkes and Loch returned. Up to the very end

[1] Elgin to Russell, 8 October, 1860.
[2] China Corr. III, pp. 181–2.

their fate was uncertain, and Loch and Parkes both declared that, on the information of a great official, their death sentence was on its way from the Emperor's scene of retirement in the north, Jehol, and that another quarter of an hour would have seen all Elgin's efforts unavailing. He had been grappling with an adversary, rational only in parts of its impossible constitution. His judgment had been perfect, but the success of his negotiations so far as the prisoners were concerned, had in the last resort been due to chance.

The prisoners, or at least those of them still alive, came back, Peking was in the hands of the allies, the Chinese government in the person of Kung had determined on unconditional surrender. But the mission, and more especially the British chief, were determined that at this, the beginning of full diplomatic relations with an oriental court, a deed of mingled treachery and inhumanity should be marked as unspeakable and never to be repeated. They had in mind, not mere formal pride, or any selfish advantage for the West. Irrevocably, for better or worse, East and West were to meet in future in trade and politics. In the interest of both sides, and of the future as well as of the present, an unmistakable lesson should be taught. So the name of the Earl of Elgin will be forever linked with the burning down of the summer palace of the Chinese Emperor. His decision has been attacked, sometimes by æsthetic critics, sometimes by the friends of humanity. To the first it must plainly be said that perfect honour and honesty, and the peace and happiness which flow from these are more beautiful things than any work of man's hands, and Elgin's act was committed in the interests of good faith and peace. To the second Elgin gave in his despatch to Lord John Russell a sufficient answer.[1] He was convinced that the Chinese, and even Prince Kung, were not yet aware of the enormity of their conduct. They must receive a lesson, in the interests of Chinese political morality. But the lesson was one which must be inflicted speedily, for the commanders now spoke of 1 November as the date on which their forces must withdraw. It could not be in the form of a great fine, for this was not a matter to be solved by money payments, and in any case China was poor enough already. It was useless to ask for the punishment of the culprits, for that, said Elgin, would only have meant the surrender of " some miserable subordinates, whom it would have been difficult to pardon, and impossible to punish."

[1] Elgin to Russell, 25 October, 1860. The arguments of the despatch seem conclusive as to Elgin's wisdom in exacting a penalty, at once severe and yet innocuous to the general population.

"I came to the conclusion that the destruction of the Yuen Ming Yuen was the least objectionable of the several courses open to me, unless I could have reconciled it to my sense of duty to suffer the crime which had been committed to pass practically unavenged. . . . It was the Emperor's favourite residence, and its destruction could not fail to be a blow to his pride as well as to his feelings. To this place he brought our hapless countrymen in order that they might undergo their severest tortures within its precincts. There have been found the horses and accoutrements of the troopers seized, the decorations torn from the breast of a gallant French officer, and other effects belonging to the prisoners. The punishment was one which would fall, not on the people, who may be comparatively innocent, but exclusively on the Emperor, whose direct personal responsibility for the crime committed is established not only by the treatment of the prisoners at Yuen Ming Yuen, but also by the edict in which he offers a pecuniary reward for the heads of the foreigners, adding that he is ready to expend all his treasure in these wages of assassination."

These chapters will have been written in vain, if they have not made it clear beyond dispute that mercy and justice to the people of China, and infinite compassion for their sufferings, were of the very essence of Lord Elgin's policy. Even in this act of stern punishment it is not an error to see the same characteristic, given its abnormal form by the mingled folly and cruelty of the court crimes and blunders. The fall of Peking, and the burning of the Summer Palace reduce the remaining unspectacular but important events of the mission to a kind of anti-climax. On 26 October the Treaty and Convention were ratified with every possible solemn ceremony—the convention containing two new clauses, one concerning coolie emigration, the other with reference to the cession of Kowloon. On the 27th, in the fitness of things, the ambassador of Great Britain took up residence in Peking in the palace of the very Prince Tsai who had been involved in the treachery of 17-18 September. All that now remained was to await the publication of the decree by which the Emperor would declare the treaties law through China, and to introduce Frederick Bruce, who had been summoned post haste, as the ambassador for Great Britain at Peking.

It has been contended that by failing to secure a personal interview with the Emperor, Lord Elgin placed a stumbling block in the way of all his successors at Peking. The criticism hardly stands the test of fact. There are many plausible arguments excusing the omission ; that Prince Kung was the government *de facto* and Kung had acknowledged not only the ambassador extraordinary of Great Britain, but the regular ambassador Frederick Bruce, with every legal courtesy ; or that in achieving a great advance in the diplomatic status of Western powers in Peking it was not possible for the powers to secure every conceivable demand ; but the decisive answer comes from the two commanders-in-chief.

273

It was essential, if the British envoy were indeed to meet the Chinese Emperor in solemn state, that the armies to which he and his French colleague had owed their diplomatic success, should remain un-diminished to support his dignity. Now the Emperor was distant from the capital, and in so ceremonious an empire it was impossible to arrange for a conference with the head of the State with the ease and lack of state with which ten years later Bismarck and Napoleon III were to meet after Sedan. Time and circumstance were essentials ; but neither Montauban nor Hope Grant could give time. Montauban was already off, having refused to wait beyond 1 November. Hope Grant had been persuaded to risk another week's delay, but he warned Elgin that the 7th or 8th of November was " the latest possible date to which I can remain, according to the best information I can obtain."[1] All the troops, with the exception of those condemned to occupy Tientsin, must be clear of Tientsin and Taku before winter closed the Peiho ; and it is confirmatory of the British commander's judgment that Lord Elgin as he made his way on 27 November to his vessel reported that he had to plough his way through ice until the Taku forts were reached and that on the bar of the river " there was so much broken ice on the inner side

[1] Hope Grant to Elgin, 29 October, 1860.

274

of it that it reminded one of some of the pictures of the arctic voyages."[1]

Before he left, Lord Elgin had installed his brother in his Embassy, giving place to him, as now the representative of Britain, in the presence of Prince Kung. His last decision was to consent that Frederick Bruce should follow the example of the French and Russian ministers, and for the moment not occupy the legation at Peking, an understudy holding the fort until a more convenient season. On 14 November Lord Elgin was at Tientsin, and on the 27th he rejoined his ship the *Ferooz*. December he spent at Shanghai, reading there among other things Darwin's *Origin of Species*, which he thought audacious.[2] Early in the new year he went to Hong-Kong to settle matters concerning Canton and Kowloon, and on 21 January, 1861, he sailed for home by Manila : the Government lending him H.M.S. *Terrible* to convey him from Alexandria to Trieste, whence he passed home through Vienna and Paris.

So ended the second of two missions to China the consequences of which to British trade and diplomatic relations with the Far East were to be as far-reaching and important in that sphere, as his government in Canada had been in the region of colonial self-government.

[1] Letters to Lady Elgin, 27 November, 1860
[2] *Ibid.*, 31 December, 1860.

CHAPTER VII

INDIA, 1862–63

THE shadow of India had fallen across Lord Elgin's career, even before he had arrived home from China. As early as May, 1860, Lord Canning had gone over the list of possible successors to himself, and, while he counted Sidney Herbert the best of all the men he knew, he had given Elgin his modified approval. Curiously enough, so little had his contemporaries understood the resolution and fixity of purpose which Lord Elgin veiled under his diplomatic reserve, that Canning thought he would " sail with the wind," counting that, however, not a bad thing for India so long as men's passions were not raised.[1] In 1861, the question of the succession to the viceroyalty had become practical politics, and Granville, when reporting on 9 April that Lord Elgin was expected to arrive that day, added that he would probably be sent to India. In July he told Canning that " Elgin will be the man," and added that he

[1] *Life of Lord Granville :* Canning to Granville, 29 May, 1860.

believed the appointment would not be disagreeable to his correspondent.[1]

One may date Lord Elgin's first acute perception of Indian problems from the letter which he wrote in 1857 at Calcutta, where, as an outsider, he watched the first impact of the Mutiny panic on Anglo-Indian society :

" It is a terrible business, this living among inferior races. I have seldom from man or woman since I came to the East heard a sentence which was reconcilable with the hypothesis that Christianity had ever come into the world. Detestation, contempt, ferocity, vengeance, whether Chinamen or Indians be the object. There are some three or four hundred servants in this house. When one first passes by their *salaaming* one feels a little awkward. But the feeling soon wears off, and one moves among them with perfect indifference, treating them, not as dogs, because in that case one would whistle to them and pat them, but as machines with which one can have no communion or sympathy. Of course those who speak the language are somewhat more *en rapport* with the natives, but very slightly so, I take it. When the passions of fear and hatred are engrafted on this indifference, the result is frightful, an absolute callousness as to the sufferings of the objects of those passions which must be witnessed to be understood and believed."[2]

And now, leaving his home for what was to prove the last time, Lord Elgin came, on 12 March, 1862,

[1] *Life of Lord Granville :* Granville to Canning, 9 April, 1861 ; and 17 July, 1861.

[2] Letters to Lady Elgin, 21 August, 1857.

to submit himself to the test of governing as a despot.

The history of the twenty months, from March, 1862, to November, 1863, was, except for events in Afghanistan, wonderfully normal and unexciting. Yet it was a period which marked a fresh starting point in Anglo-Indian history, and no one can study the career of Elgin in India, broken and incomplete as it is, without feeling that, even more than Cornwallis in the eighteenth century, he was peculiarly fitted to give Anglo-Indian administration a new orientation. India, as it passed from Canning's hands to those of Elgin, was a land of problems. It had reached the transition stage, when the days of company rule were passing into those of modern politics. No doubt, as Elgin told the Queen, India was " at peace in a sense of the term more emphatic and comprehensive than it had ever before borne in India " ; [1] but for the Viceroy it was a troubled peace.

To begin with, it was impossible for the relation of races to remain in the condition of unnatural strain which not even Canning's clemency could quite relieve. The English civilian population either found it difficult to assume an easy attitude towards the world which had so recently threatened to destroy them, or it began to speculate

[1] Lord Elgin to the Queen, 20 January, 1863.

whether government could not help them to draw
selfish advantages from the military prostration
which had overwhelmed the rebels. Would the
new viceroy be able, in India, to repeat his tran-
quillizing successes in Jamaica and Canada?

The mere machinery of government, too, required
careful consideration and much readjustment. The
acts of 1853, 1858 and 1861, and the work of Dalhousie and Canning presented Elgin with a curious
mosaic of old and new. The company directors
had gone, and the Crown was now supreme : but
the position of the new Secretary of State had still
to be defined, both as an isolated office, and as the
centre of the Council which threatened in many
ways to repeat the example of the vanished director-
ate. What exactly was the nature of the authority
of the " Secretary of State in Council " ? Was
the Viceroy more or less powerful than the Governor-General had been, and would British Parliamentary interest in India act as a friendly support,
an aggressive critic, or a supplanting power?

There was Dalhousie's legislative council too,
with its open debates, and its ill-defined position.
Here lay possibilities of development into a kind
of unofficial parliament for India ; but it was also
possible to regard it as a troublesome and unessential
debating society, encumbering the real government,
the Governor-General in Council. And especially

with men like Bartle Frere at Bombay and Montgomery in the Punjab, some careful definition was
required delimiting the frontiers of the central and
the provincial authorities. As has always happened
in constitutional development, these were for Elgin
not abstract legal questions, but intensely personal
facts. At home, his secretary was Sir Charles
Wood, an experienced hand in Indian affairs, with
a powerful council, chief among whom was John
Lawrence, the predominant figure in the late crisis,
whose iron will and great experience would surrender freedom to the Viceroy with some reluctance.
At Simla Sir Hugh Rose lay encamped with all the
prestige of his Mutiny campaigns, and all the
willingness of a soldier to dictate terms to an inex-
perienced civilian. The council at Calcutta with
its semi-independent departmental heads, its set
bureaucratic ways, its internecine domestic feuds,
and its gift of writing minutes, might easily and at
any moment create trouble at home, in the provinces, and with the Governor-General himself. A
troublesome financial member, Laing, was on the
point of taking flight (to continue his controversies
at home), and Elgin was a little startled to find that
Wood was sending out, as his successor, Trevelyan,
whose previous departure from India had been the
result of action towards the Governor-General which
was both injudicious and hardly constitutional.

As for the presidencies and provinces, Frere's great capacity, and endless energy, and restless opinionativeness, meant that whatever regions failed to gain its rights, Bombay would not lose hers for want of agitating. And in the Punjab, there was not only the natural tendency of the border provinces to push forward, but the existence of some groups of men, as noble in character, and capable in action as any in English history, but all of them with individual characteristics abnormally developed, and contemptuous of the sedentary gentlemen who ruled from Calcutta. The Calvinistic evangelicalism of men like Macleod and Edwardes, nourished by a life of strenuous action, and provoked to openness by a Mohammedan creed not unlike their own, threatened at any moment to excite religious passions in India, and ecclesiastical rhetoric in Exeter Hall.[1]

Machinery apart, the administrative work ahead of Elgin hardly promised him leisure and quiet. The finance of the English dominion in India had never quite conformed to business methods.

---

[1] It is plain from Lord Elgin's correspondence that one of the chief reasons why Herbert Edwardes was never given the chance to fulfil the startling promise of his early days was the distrust in his judgment which his religious fervour bred at headquarters.

Deficits had been the rule : expenses, in spite of all reductions since repression of the Mutiny, had been as expansive as the revenue had been stationary : and Wilson and Laing, whom the Home government had sent out to retrieve earlier errors, created some fresh difficulties. Yet, on the face of it all, India was crying for financial development. Not only roads, but tramways and railways had to be built, canals extended, and irrigation pushed ahead. Medical and sanitary knowledge, penetrating last of all into army medical circles, was beginning to reveal scandals in the housing of the troops, and the inadequacy of existing barracks. To crown all, Lancashire was in straits for want of cotton—the American civil war was at its height— and, with some disregard for Indian conditions, English commercial interests were assailing both home and Indian authorities, and demanding doubtful and occasionally fantastic advantages.

" No doubt," wrote Elgin to his former financial minister, " we have a service to England and the world in the matter of cotton ; but when we observe the preposterous character of the proposals for effecting the object, made to us by persons who used to enjoy a reputation for commonsense and fairness,—such proposals for example as that the government of India should buy up all the cotton in the country, and transport it to the seaboard on the chance of its finding a market there,—we cannot but feel that the prospect of satisfying expectations on this head is far from encouraging."[1]

Finally there was the eternal problem of the North-West, with its fanatic or marauding tribes, the kaleidoscopic fortunes of Afghan and Persian politics, and the thunder-cloud of Russian advance on the remote horizon. War, or even a spirited border policy, meant heavy deficits, and declining public works. But, even if war could be avoided, there must always be doubtful reflections on the advantages of masterly inactivity.

It will clarify this examination of Elgin's work, if the few main dates in his short period of rule be kept in mind. He was installed in Calcutta on 12 March, 1862 ; and continued in or near that city till 5 February, 1863. During that time, the most important events for him were the arrivals of Mr. (later Sir Henry) Maine in November, 1862, and of Sir C. Trevelyan early in January, 1863, as members of Council, and of his wife on 8 January. He left Calcutta, never again to see it, in February : visited Benares, Allahabad, Cawnpore, Agra, Delhi, Umballa and other places, holding Durbars, making speeches, and gathering facts and opinions as he progressed, and reached Simla on

[1] Elgin to Laing, 9 September, 1862. Elgin and Wood deserve some credit for postponing the date at which " government by business men " began.

4 April, 1863. Parallel with these events, the operations of Dost Mohammed in Afghanistan were keeping his Foreign Department awake, until in July, 1863, he was able to report that the fall of Herat need not involve India in trouble, and that rumour had it that the Ameer was dead.

On 26 September he left Simla on his last march, intending to go to Peshawur : and almost at once news from the Punjab forced him to authorize his one armed expedition, against the Sitana fanatics on the upper Indus. He had been, from time to time, unwell, but the marches in the upland regions and his adventures in October proved too much for him. His last letter to Sir Charles Wood, on 4 November, suggested doubts as to his power of continuing to do his duty. He died on 20 November. On that same day Sir Neville Chamberlain was wounded in desperate defensive fighting, on the Sitana expedition which the Governor-General had authorized.

The foundation of Elgin's work lay in the establishment of sound relations between white and brown under his rule. As has been seen, the position was still abnormal, and in any case a white aristocracy is seldom just or merciful to its subjects. On this point Secretary of State and Governor-General were at one. Wood condensed his view into two sharp sentences : " I consider it my duty

THE EARL AND COUNTESS OF ELGIN AND THEIR DAUGHTER, LADY LOUISA BRUCE, AT SIMLA 1863.

to protect the native, and I shall say so most dis-
tinctly " [1] ; and again : " I have a great fear when
white men make exceptional laws for white masters
against black servants." [2] Some of Canning's legislation had displeased him from this point of view,
and he left Elgin in no doubt as to his sentiments :

" There is another bill," he wrote about a Contract
law which seemed to violate British standards of justice,
" which I beg you to keep back till you hear from us—
the Fraudulent Contract bill. It seems to me, as it
stands, to be monstrous. I sent it to Sir George Grey,
who looked it over with Waddington at the H.O., and
says it could not be tolerated here. But in India such a
bill is in one respect more objectionable, for the purpose
to which it is to be applied is to imprison black men at
the suit of whites ; and the precedent aptly quoted in the
government despatch is the legislation of a *slave* State
in America. There may be some reason for dealing with
a fraudulent breach of contract in a different mode from
what is applied to a mere failure to perform, but certainly
hard labour on the roads, and possible whipping if the
debtor does not work hard enough, is a very new feature
in the law as applicable to debtor and creditor." [3]

Elgin, however, required no prompting, even in
the more acutely difficult cases presented to him
on the spot. He could boast, as few others then
could, that during a public service of twenty years
he had always sided with the weaker party. Now,
as always, he was resolute to prevent violation of

[1] Wood to Elgin, 17 November, 1862.
[2] *Ibid.*, 9 January, 1863.   [3] *Ibid.*, 9 August, 1862.

local feelings in matters of religion and traditional sentiment, and he proved extraordinarily jealous of missionary extravagance, checking at once the over-evangelical inclinations of his North-West frontier men. He was quite merciless in individual cases of outrage or murder. In one case where a soldier, Rudd, had wantonly slain a native who was legitimately defending his property, and in which public opinion inclined to petition for his reprieve, he took matters quietly into his own hands :

" The verdict was clearly borne out by the evidence. The sentence was in accordance with the law, and the judge, to whom I referred, saw no reason to question it. The decision of the Governor-General in Council was that the law must take its course."[1]

In another, where an officer had behaved with frightful brutality to a servant suspected of theft, Elgin, after recounting the case with expressions of disgust, reported to Wood that the culprit was to be tried by a general court-martial.[2]

He cut deeper into the difficulty than this. He knew that half the injustice and mercilessness came from panic, and panic from rumours listened to with foolish credulity. The European community was, perhaps not unnaturally, afflicted with recur-

---

[1] Elgin to Wood, 22 June, 1862.
[2] *Ibid.*, 17 August, 1862.

rent epidemics of plot and massacre rumours. With a certain Scottish grimness of humour Elgin himself reported a plan for his own assassination. It was necessary to check the habit among the leaders of opinion, and chance handed over no less a person than the Commander-in-Chief for treatment.

Sir Hugh Rose, not knowing his man, and subject to the prevalent military inclination to alarmist rumours, enclosed a most interesting and preposterous bundle of soldiers' reports for the Governor-General's perusal. " Strange rumours circulate from village to village," reported one officer, " and the common cultivators know not what exactly to expect, *but are looking for a something* " [1] ; and the rest of Rose's information was in the same key. Elgin's reply was a masterpiece of quiet contemptuous disapproval, and thereafter the Commander-in-Chief's correspondence lost in interest what it gained in common sense :

" I am much obliged to you for the letters which you have sent me, containing copies of statements received by you from different persons, on the subject of Persian intrigues in Herat, Mahomedan disaffection in India, etc., etc. I cannot say that I form a very high estimate of the strength of nerve and political sagacity of some of your informants, and of those who supply the reports which they transmit. Nevertheless I think it advisable

---

[1] Wheler to Sir Hugh Rose, 2 June, 1862.

that all that is to be said on such matters should be heard, and I shall thankfully accept any communication which you may forward to me, from time to time, from whatever quarter they emanate. As regards the subject matter of these speculations, I suppose that we all know that our presence in India is regarded with dislike by Mahomedans in general, Persia in particular, and by a good many others who are more or less concealed from view. We know, moreover, that this dislike is constantly embodying itself in designs, more or less shadowy, which have our expulsion for their object. From this conviction, however, to the adoption of measures which may compromise our finances by entailing on us heavy expenditure, and our dignity by making us parties to intrigues, which we can neither control nor fathom, is a very wide interval. Before we attempt to bridge it, we must satisfy ourselves that the foundation on which we are about to build is sound."[1]

On the whole, the most vital question touched on by Elgin in India concerned the relation of the different parts of the government to each other. Here he was without question the greatest master of constitutional practice in the empire at that time. A comparison between the working government of Canada, say in 1867, and that of any other self-governing colony, will reveal the immense superiority in *working* qualities of the Canadian constitution. Now Elgin had been, more than any other single man, the political expert who had begun the shaping of that instrument of govern-

[1] Elgin to Sir Hugh Rose, 20 March, 1863.

ment. Political problems in India were no doubt very different, and there were highly intelligent experts like Bartle Frere and John Lawrence ready primed with their opinions founded on long Eastern experience. But that in which Lord Elgin differed from all others was that he had at once the leverage and the responsibility of his position, and a store of general constitutional experience such as no other statesman connected with India possessed : and, in addition, he had an instinct for avoiding lop-sided views.

One or two unessential but troublesome bad habits in government fretted him. His natural inclinations and his earlier experiences both set him against the bureaucratic habit of mind. He disliked the irresponsible independence of the Anglo-Indian officials, their cut-and-dried certainty, their spinster-like political decorum, and, perhaps most of all, the ill-temper and ill-manners of their ordinary procedure. At once he protested against the senseless friction which existed between different parts of the Indian machinery, department challenging department, and lieutenant-governors the central authority : and he disliked the factious publicity sought by some of the disputants : " The extent to which the public and the press here are invited to take part in the domestic disputes which occur from time to time between branches of the government strikes a new-comer as somewhat strange."[1] He was especially annoyed at the effect of English action in "sending out a chancellor of the exchequer on the openly avowed plea that the Governor-General in Council was incapable of performing aright without his aid the most important function of government,"[2] and still more annoyed when one of these improvised chancellors proceeded to adopt, first in India, and then in England, the most modern methods of political propaganda.

But the central question concerned the position of the Viceroy. The later acts of Lord Canning had provoked the Home government into a vigorous assertion of its supremacy, and repeated protests against publishing measures without any reference home.

"It is all wrong," the Secretary of State wrote. "Many occasions require instant action, or are not very important. Here are two, one of which affects the future revenue of India for ever ; the other is a matter in which English experience is great, and Indian experience none ; and in both the government of India acts without waiting for the opinion of the government at home. This is not right ; and it is not wise. The Home government is the absolute power, and strong as its disposition may be to support the government in India (as it ought), there

---

[1] Elgin to Wood, 23 March, 1862.

[2] Referring to the appointments first of Wilson, and then of Laing to the Financial Department.

are limits to that. In details, and urgent matters, the government of India ought to do everything, but in matters of *principle* it ought to be sure of the support of the Home government ; and it is foolish if it does not ensure that before it acts."[1]

The sinner here was, of course, not Elgin, but Canning.

The new Viceroy did not acquiesce in the situation, feeling indeed that Wood's statements barely covered the situation. For one thing he found that, whoever was master, Wood and his Council were hardly playing the game, resorting as a regular habit to the collection of information, from unauthorized sources, behind the Governor-General's back. " Most of your councillors," he wrote, " have correspondents out here, who pass judgment on what happens, with the freedom characteristic of the verdict of persons who are themselves irresponsible, and very imperfectly acquainted with the notions of those whom they criticize."[2] He might have added that local potentates, like Frere at Bombay, were accustomed to correspond at least as freely with the India Office as with the Governor-General in support of measures presumably the business of Calcutta and not Westminster. Apart,

[1] Wood to Elgin, 9 April, 1862.
[2] Elgin to Wood, 9 September, 1862. In Canada Elgin had been plagued by the same ill-habit, especially at the hands of Churchmen, and he always resented it.

however, from such errors in practice, Elgin had a curiously modern feeling that the chief power must lie with the Governor-General, and that undue interference from London was bad policy. He saw that not only must he be firm in asserting his power, but that far more prudence and consideration were necessary at home.

" Between the Secretary of State who, necessarily, as *The Times* says, represents the Great Mogul, and the little moguls, the local governors, who hold the doctrine that the interference of the supreme government is not only a nuisance but indefensible in principle, because it militates against the practice of local self-government, the question of whether there be any legitimate sphere of action for the government of India, and if there be, what that sphere of action is, naturally suggests itself for consideration."[1]

He compared the power left to him at Calcutta with that which Canadian self-government had left him at Quebec :

" If I were to tell you what I *now* think of the relative amount of influence which I exercised on the march of affairs in Canada, where I governed on strictly constitutional principles, and with a free parliament, as compared with that which the Governor-General wields in India, when at peace, you would accuse me of paradox."[2]

The real danger was that, in the East, where prestige and the appearance of power count for so

[1] Elgin to Wood, 5 March, 1863.
[2] *Ibid.*, 9 December, 1862.

much, the usefulness of the viceroyalty might
suffer. In his short term of office Elgin certainly
surrendered nothing due to his office. He was
master, even in his departments, and even over
Trevelyan at the Treasury. He kept Bartle Frere
in proper perspective and proportion, although he
gave Bombay most of what Frere thought it should
have. The Commander-in-Chief ultimately approached his superior with becoming deference.
What the ultimate relationship with the British
Government would have been one cannot say ; but
it is plain that Elgin's ideas on the relative positions
of Secretary of State and Governor-General corresponded much more to those of recent reforms
than to the parliamentarianism of Sir Charles
Wood. Had life and energy been granted him,
so accomplished a diplomat in constitutional mysteries would almost certainly have, on the one hand,
controlled his bureaucrats by his skill in personal
management, and on the other, asserted as vigorously as even Frere could have desired, that India
must be governed in India. Whether he would
have been right is a different question.

Another interesting and most modern point at
issue concerned the Governor-General's council.
Dalhousie had developed a legislative council,
which was the Governor-General in Council with
certain additions. The proceedings of this body

were public property. Again, in 1861, Wood, Canning, and Frere had modified the constitution of this body, although Wood had acted with great reluctance, believing, as he told Frere, that " representative bodies, in any real sense, you cannot have, and I do not think that any external element will *really do good*."[1] Wood lost no time in reminding the new Governor-General how things stood.

" You have a council which occasionally makes laws, and when it makes laws certain other people sit with your ordinary councillors. But your council is one and the same council ; and we took very great pains throughout the act to avoid any word which could favour the action of the separate existence of a legislative council. It had been improperly so constituted by Dalhousie, and we took great pains to undo his mistake."[2]

More emphatically he wrote, with frequent underlinings, " Let me point out to you that you have NO LEGISLATIVE COUNCIL."[3]

Elgin, who was profoundly cautious in constitutional affairs until he could see some distance ahead, bowed to the storm ; but his mind began to work on the problem, and continued to work till the end. There is a danger here, as with the viceroyalty, of reading modern developments into

[1] Martineau, *Life of Frere*, I, 336.
[2] Wood to Elgin, 19 May, 1862.
[3] *Ibid.*, 10 May, 1862 : The double emphasis is from Wood's own pen.

mid-Victorian practice. But the final impression left by a study of Elgin's letters to all his official correspondents is that he welcomed the idea of the additional, and especially of the non-official, legislative councillors, and that, had he lived, the legislative council would have found encouragement, and seen development, at his hands. Wood had made light of the whole affair, and refused to allow the use of terms like " session " and " adjournment " in dealing with it. But the constitutional good sense of Elgin saw that, after all, important people had been summoned to the meetings in question, and that it was impossible to ignore what was an actual fact.

" In talking of the prorogation of the council I have hitherto used the word ' adjournment,' but as the word ' session ' occurs in the rules, I suppose that I must correct my phraseology and employ the former designation. I do not think that it much matters which term is used. An interruption of the sittings, in whatever language you define it, must take place. The supreme council contains, and necessarily contains, members, unofficial members, chiefly natives, from remote parts of India. Is it possible to require them to remain permanently absent from their homes ? And if that be impossible, would it be decorous or judicious, to say to them, ' You may go, and we shall get on just as well without as with you.' If you make them members, it is a great deal better to act on the presumption that their presence and assistance, while the work of legislation is in progress, is desirable, and therefore to arrange so as to make it at least possible for them to give it. These can only be effected by the adoption of some system of sessions or long adjournments."[1]

Latterly he was immensely attracted by the idea of holding sessions of this council at different points of importance in India, other than Calcutta, or the hills. There was a perpetual debate as to the proper seat of government for all India ; and Elgin thought that some at least of the difficulties would be met by these peripatetic legislative council meetings. He gave great attention not only to the choice of suitable new members of the council, but equally to the choice of a suitable centre for the meeting. In choosing Lahore as the centre for meeting in January, 1864, he obviously meant to use the whole idea for important ulterior ends in the government of India. He spoke to Sir C. Trevelyan about " the experiment of popularizing the council of the Governor-General, and giving it a more catholic character." Especially to his heads of departments—men like Napier or Trevelyan—he wrote much, in the months before his collapse, about the coming events. " I attach, for reasons which you will appreciate, great importance to our assembly at Lahore this winter," he wrote to Napier. " I have arranged to have there a camp

[1] Elgin to Wood, 19 April, 1862.

of exercise of some 12,000 men ; and it is desirable that this military display should be qualified by a meeting for peaceful and political objects, at which some of the principal Sikh chiefs may play a prominent part."[1] His mind was so obviously working on the subject, in the later part of 1863, and he had so plainly betrayed his view that the meeting at Lahore must prove important, that we must consider his policy for the future of the legislative council as being something very different from Wood's unwilling recognition of the pale phantom to which he even denied the name of council.

Space forbids further detailed examination of Elgin's constitutional views, but sufficient has been said to show how acutely his mind was working on problems of the machinery of Indian government. It is not mere fantasy to say that, had he lived, his regime might well have marked one of the great stages in advance in Indian constitutional reform. The administrative and financial aspects of Lord Elgin's rule demand less attention than do his constitutional reflections and experiments ; for, although viceroys in India stand or fall mainly on their administrative record, Elgin had little time in which to master the routine details of his work, and to add those complementary touches which would have constituted his own contribution. In

[1] Elgin to Sir R. Napier, 20 August, 1863.

any case, nothing is so dead as the details of old budgets and programmes of public works. But there are some interesting hints and fragments of a policy which suggest what he might have done, had he lived.

He inherited from Canning an imperfectly clarified situation—half of it consisting of old confusions, deficits and projects, the other half, the reforms and innovations of Wilson and Laing, the two British financiers sent in succession to rectify the earlier financial chaos. There was a series of problems to be answered. A budget had to be constructed which would show a surplus : and in that budget some decision must be come to as to the customs duties and the income tax which provided the adjustable items. Lancashire desired to see the import duties lowered or abolished : Anglo-Indians like Trevelyan and others of the Council longed to end at once the income tax, which seemed to them one of Wilson's least appropriate Western ideas. The governments of the provinces, and more especially Frere at Bombay, were crying out for money to spend on public works, especially roads, railways and irrigation schemes : while, at the centre, the watch-dogs of the treasury snarled at all presumptuous efforts to make off with their treasures. There were conveniently obscure phrases like " cash balances," and " loss by exchange " which helped to confuse the financier as he balanced his accounts. Some decision must be arrived at concerning the fate of Canning's projects for waste land sales and the redemption of land revenues : and English speculators must be taught that India existed for purposes more serious than to assist their profiteering. In all these matters the Secretary of State claimed at least his reasonable share of influence ; and Elgin was just a little startled to learn that his new financial member was to be Trevelyan, whose injudicious action over the imposition of an income tax, had ended his career at Madras, and whom Macaulay, whose evidence here is relevant, had described as " almost always on the right side in every question ; and it is well that he is so, for he gives a most confounded deal of trouble when he happens to take the wrong one."[1]

It was Elgin's natural way, and in any case much the wisest thing he could have done, to receive suggestions from all sides—Bartle Frere's enthusiastic demands for public works in Bombay : Wood's varying but always forcible injunctions to do nothing without consulting the Home government, but to pile up his public works, and defer the paying off of debts : Trevelyan's fresh and general ideas, especially on the income tax. His cool sense

[1] Trevelyan, *Life of Lord Macaulay*, c. vi.

helped to dispel a few illusions. Whether he was, or was not, to spend his cash balances, he wished his colleagues to understand what these actually were. "How can the sums which stand at our credit under this head," he wrote rather sharply to Wood, "be essentially anything but *an accumulation of monies owed by us,* when in point of fact our expenditure during past years has almost always exceeded our income?" In face of the willingness of Trevelyan, and of Anglo-Indians in general, to neglect, in their balance-sheet, the item of "loss by exchange," he told them that they must face the fact. He withdrew the opposition of Calcutta to Frere's Bombay projects for public works, but with a touch of humour he warned that irrepressible enthusiast : "To your declaration, perfectly borne out, no doubt, by the facts, ' We must have a great deal of money, for we could spend it to great advantage,' I add the proviso, ' You shall have it, if we have it to give, but not otherwise.' "

His, or rather Trevelyan's first effort at a Budget had the good luck to secure an unexpected surplus ; but his term of office terminated before one can really say what he would or would not have done to develop the finances and prosperity of India. Even more than Dalhousie he was a believer in modern inventions, and he desired to see India economize labour and spare unnecessary friction, whether in the substitution of trains for beasts of burden, or in devices for the cooling of the air in houses. As he very shrewdly remarked to Wood, "Although we are dealing here with a very old country, it is in many particulars as respects progress and development as virgin as young America." He therefore thought that, in opening up fresh tracts for traffic, the government might imitate the U.S.A. in using "the means of locomotion which the nineteenth century has provided, without thinking it necessary to establish alongside of them, for purposes of competition, roads and conveyances which may have been thought excellent at the date of the Heptarchy."[1]

In this administrative region he may perhaps best be gauged by the letter which he wrote to the Secretary of State immediately after Sir Charles Trevelyan arrived : it is the clearest indication he ever gave of anything like a programme :

"I have had a good deal of conversation with Trevelyan. He is very friendly, and I think disposed to act in the best spirit. In some respects I confess that I thought his views rather crude. There appeared to me to be a disposition to treat imaginary surpluses a little too much as if they were actually in his pocket, a loose way of assuming that our revenue *must* go on rapidly increasing from year to year, which somewhat alarmed me. It is fair however to say that he met my cautions on this head

[1] Elgin to Wood, 19 October, 1862.

by explaining that he was arguing on such hypothetical data, only because he did not expect me to be within reach at the time when the actual results of the financial year would be in his possession, and because he wished by previous communication with me to prepare himself for all contingencies. This may be quite true, but, unless I am much mistaken, no man would have used the language on these subjects which he employed in conversation with me, who had not a sanguine and somewhat speculative temperament. Now, where you have to pass your measures through the ordeal of free assemblies, where all opinions are represented and have a voice, a sanguine, and even a somewhat speculative temperament may be useful, perhaps indispensable to the attainment of great ends. Nor do I affirm that it will prove a bad thing even here, but under a system such as that of India, and in administering the affairs of a community so intolerant of novelty in taxation, any tendency to abandon existing sources of revenue on speculative anticipations of increase, must be carefully kept in check. . . . I told him that, for my part, I should be very well satisfied if the financial results of his first year of administration were as follows :

" Firstly : a confirmation of the public mind in the belief that the income tax will be allowed to drop at the close of the five years for which it was originally enacted.

" Secondly : a liberal appropriation for public works and education, the appropriations for the former of these objects, in so far as the works are reproductive, being in my judgment in the nature of a sinking fund.

" Thirdly : a real surplus of income over charge on the transactions of the year, including in the charge the appropriations from revenue for public works, whether reproductive or otherwise ; but excluding, of course, any outlay on such works of funds taken avowedly from the cash balances. I am strongly of opinion that if all this was shown unequivocally on the face of our year's business, it would tend to raise our credit far more than any peddling attempts to reduce taxes which nobody cares very much about."[1]

In Indian politics one comes sooner or later to foreign policy, which always means the North-West frontier, and usually drags in Russia. Happily, in Lord Elgin's case, Russia does not appear, and, while there is no novelty in his diplomatic record, there is a sense of certainty and completeness, to be found in no other department of his government. Here he knew exactly what he wanted ; he had a specific problem or two to face, and he did exactly what he intended.

Like all the Liberal-Conservatives of the Peel and Aberdeen school, he was judiciously pacific : which meant that he sought peace, not as a dogma, but as a useful and helpful fact. But while he always roused the fire-eaters, whether in Canada, or China, or India, to easy indignation, he could prove very stiff when the situation so demanded. As the burning of the Peking summer palace proved, he was a master of judicious severity. Early in his Indian career he invited Holkar to conform to the strict usages of imperial diplomacy in his communications with England. Twice he had occasion to discipline

[1] Elgin to Wood, 20 January, 1863.

the ruler of Nepal. When on his high diplomatic horse he did not even spare the British Government, and seized the opportunity when it presented itself to give Wood a lesson in diplomatic methods, pointing out firmly that it was not advisable that the Secretary of State should communicate with the native chiefs otherwise than through the government of India.[1]

On the main business of his foreign policy, however, he was completely at one with his minister. Those were days when John Lawrence's word carried chief weight in the India Office, and before Disraeli felt himself qualified to educate the chief experts in Indian affairs. Masterly inactivity was the word, and it was the right word. Dost Mohammed had designs on Herat, and Persia had corresponding fears. If an Afghan advance on Herat should be pushed too far, Persia would be able to claim, under treaty rights, the good offices of England. Again, when the Dost died, there would be the usual struggle for the throne, and chances of the Afghan troubles spreading. As a matter of fact, everything happened as the prophets of evil forecast. Dost Mohammed captured both Furrah and Herat ; the Persian government worked itself into wild excitement ; Dost Mohammed died ; and there were successive troubles. But thanks to the

[1] Elgin to Wood, 9 May, 1862.

perfect understanding between Wood and Elgin, and to the calm wisdom of Elgin's action in India, the strife was localized and ended where it began.

Wood, instructed by men like Napier and Lawrence, knew his own mind :

" I am for letting the Afghans fight it out among themselves. The Dost may annex Herat. I really do not think that it signifies to us one anna. It is more probable that at his death the whole Afghan concern will fall to pieces again, and it seems to me waste of time to trouble ourselves about the present state, or *any* present state of things, which must so soon be changed by the death of the Dost."[1]

It is one of the misfortunes of a people and press trained to love melodrama that they never understand the preventive victories of sound diplomacy. Elgin entirely agreed with the home authorities. On these matters he is much his own best exponent, and his letter to the Secretary of State, 21 May, 1863, is one of the soundest documents written by him in India :

" Frere, you tell me, finds fault with our policy in Afghanistan. I have no doubt that it is considered slow by a good many of his friends at the frontier. What chances of diplomatic distinctions, and perhaps even military rewards we are foregoing ! You may remember a rather dictatorial epistle which Sir Robert Montgomery addressed to me some months ago in this strain, informing me that the time had come when I must announce the

---

[1] Wood to Elgin, 25 August, 1862.

policy of England on the Afghan question—pointing out that there were two courses only between which I must choose : that I must either say the Dost was to have Herat, or that he was not to have Herat, and that as both courses were equally objectionable it did not much matter which I preferred. I called your attention at the time to this rather crooked piece of logic. And, in point of fact, what would have been our position, if I had followed these courses ? If we had said the Dost was not to have Herat, we should have made him our enemy : perhaps thrown him into alliance with Persia. If we had said the contrary, we should have been in the eyes of Persia, Russia, etc., responsible for proceedings, which, if not violation of our engagements with Persia, trench very nearly on the breach of them. Look on the other hand at what we have actually done. When the Dost marched on Furrah, although we took no responsibility in the matter (in fact he asked neither for assistance nor advice) we allowed our vakeel to remain with him, because we considered that he had a right, if he chose, to resent the violation of his territory which had taken place. When he attacked Herat, we withdrew our vakeel, because although we did not consider this proceeding a breach of treaty, requiring our interposition, we were desirous to show that we discountenanced it. If the Dost, after taking Herat, invades Persia, we shall have a new state of things to deal with—a clear case of treaty obligation, which may warrant decided language, and action corresponding may then possibly arise. I may be wrong, but it strikes me that I shall not find it difficult to bring the Ameer double quick back to Cabul, if you would let me take my own way of doing this."

It was characteristic of this urbane Machiavelli that, when Herat was occupied, and the Ameer

notified him of the event, Elgin " expressed satisfaction with the news communicated to him, *because it put an end to hostilities which he deplored.*" He
also advised the Dost " not to give such umbrage
to Persia as would entitle that power to invoke, as
against them, our treaty engagements with it."[1]
His last step, in an entirely useful and brilliant
piece of preventive statesmanship, was to allow his
vakeel to remain with Shere Ali Khan, who had
been named by Dost Mohammed as his successor,
but to command abstention from any acts of
partisanship when the succession strife should
begin.[2]

Paradoxically enough, the career of this most
judicious of all the Viceroys of India ended with a
little war : and one in which to the civilian eye,
and in spite of some " unfortunate incidents,"
Elgin's instructions were completely justified. A
sect of Mohammedan fanatics, time and again disciplined by the frontier forces, threatened trouble
once more from their old centre, Sitana, on the
upper Indus, and Montgomery reported possible
support to them from the neighbouring tribes.
Elgin had just left Simla on his way, he hoped, to
Peshawur ; and he thought " that the interests
both of prudence and humanity would be best con-

[1] Elgin to Wood, 13 July, 1863.
[2] *Ibid.*, 14 August, 1863.

sulted by levelling a speedy and decisive blow at
the embryo conspiracy."[1] He resisted the advice
of Sir Hugh Rose who wished to postpone action,
to undertake, in spring, war on a broader basis,
and to place himself in charge of the operations.
" I wish," he told Wood, " by a sudden and vigorous
blow to check this trouble on our frontier, while it
is in a nascent condition."

Unfortunately, and the ignorance of the fact
must be blamed on the Intelligence department,
the troubles were more than nascent ; all the
neighbouring tribes rose ; Neville Chamberlain
found himself forced to act on the defensive, and
ultimately to call for more troops. But it seems to
me that Elgin was right in acting as he did : although the military authorities might have held
more troops in reserve. The time had come for
action : Chamberlain was obviously the man for
the work : although after Elgin's death, the faint
hearts of the Council wished to withdraw, the men
of action followed what would certainly have been
Elgin's plan : and, two months after the first
advance had been commenced, British troops super-
intended the destruction, by defeated tribesmen,
of Malka, the chief settlement of the fanatics, and
the frontier relapsed into its usual state of unstable
equilibrium. Meanwhile, Elgin had died on the

[1] Elgin to Wood, 4 October, 1863.

very day on which his general was fighting his most desperate battle to maintain his position among the hills.[1]

It would be singularly inappropriate to end this chapter on Lord Elgin's work in India with a panegyric. Elgin disliked perorations, except when, as with his Bostonian and Buffalonian friends, he found that men liked that fashion of conducting negotiations. He was always just, and honest, and fond of hard facts : so that one dare not pretend that his Governor-Generalship marked in itself any special epoch in Indian affairs. It stands as one of the unfinished chapters there. But this, at least, may be said. His foreign policy followed the great traditions of Clive, Hastings, Metcalfe, and Lawrence, the defensive strategists of the North-West frontier. Judged by his unusual and invariable success in managing individuals, and the clear views he held as to the rights of the Indian Governor-General, it seems likely that the Central government would have gained enormously under him, probably at the expense of the Secretary of State : and it is certain that he would have changed the legislative council into something modern and effective. In finance and progressive administration, he could hardly have fallen below the

[1] There is an excellent account of this Sitana, or Umbeyla, campaign in Forrest's *Life of Sir Neville Chamberlain*, c. 14.

greatest of his fellow governors : and in justice and mercy and calm wisdom, even as it is, he stands on the same level with Canning and John Lawrence.

One may conclude with words of his which still have some bearing on British policy in the East :

" My modest ambition for England is that she should in this Eastern world establish the reputation of being all just and all powerful. But, to achieve this object, we must cease to attempt to play a great part in small intrigues, or to dictate in cases where we have not positive interests which we can avow, or convictions sufficiently distinct to enable us to speak plainly. We must interfere only where we can put forward an unimpeachable plea of right or duty ; and when we announce a resolution, our neighbours must understand that it is the decree of fate."

*   *   *   *   *

Lord Elgin's place in British imperial history will have become apparent in this narrative of his twenty years of incessant public service. He was one of a little group of Englishmen, in every generation to be numbered rather in scores than in hundreds, whom their vocation separates from the common life of Britain without conferring on them any abiding home in the lands which they govern. These alone may be termed citizens of the empire, men doomed to a kind of eternal homesickness for a country which exists only in their dreams and through their services. They have little share in the social distinctions of the centre. Their more notable decisions are announced as measures of the minister whose department they serve ; and the crowd learns of their existence mainly through sensational versions in the press of their occasional mistakes. In the distant regions where they do their work, they seem aliens or half-aliens ; and when they challenge doubtful projects conceived by men on the spot, on their heads breaks the storm of local denunciation. Yet they, and no others, make the continuance of the empire possible.

In the middle years of the nineteenth century, before modern inventions had simplified administration by minimizing distance, but when problems of race and government had begun to assume their modern forms, three men of the group revealed qualities of statesmanship comparable to those of the greater domestic leaders, the Marquess of Dalhousie, John, Lord Lawrence, and the Earl of Elgin. These powers Lord Elgin exhibited most notably in his work in Canada. In Jamaica it had been his duty to maintain stability in an interval between two periods of revolutionary change. In China and Japan he had to blaze the trail for diplomatists and traders by arranging experimental agreements with two hostile, or at best suspicious, governments. In India, where he might have proved himself the greatest of pacific viceroys, fate allotted him too little time. But in Canada he accomplished work, complete, fundamental, and permanent. It was not merely that he made the decisive concession of responsible government. Autonomy was inevitable, although in weaker hands the final surrender might have been effected reluctantly and clumsily. It was rather that through eight years Lord Elgin learned to understand, and sympathize with the instincts, ambitions, and powers, from which the demand for self-government proceeded. Latterly he was able to anticipate his ministers' desires, and to govern Canada rather as a Canadian than as a representative of the Imperial Government. He taught Canadians the place and limits of race feeling, he led them from petty hates, and obsolete political argumentation into quieter regions of practical administration, assisted them to material prosperity, and made them think of British North America as something greater than a disconnected group of jealous provinces. Faced with the turbulence and blunders of a young democracy, he never lost faith or courage, and he believed that liberty might be trusted to complete the work which he had begun.

Seventy years of unbroken progress have justified his confidence ; and his best memorial is the young Canadian nation.

THE END

INDEX

Aberdeen, Earl of, 163
Afghanistan and N.W. frontier, 283, 284, 304–8
Andrews, I. D., 166, 171, 177–86
Arrow (lorcha), 195, 198, 201, 212

Baldwin, Robert, 92, 94, 99, 113, 114, 116, 118, 124, 148
Berkeley, Maj.-General, 77
Bowring, Sir John, 195–200
British colonization, 13–17
— — problems connected with, 17–33
— history, Elgin's place in, 7, 310
— policy in the East, Elgin's idea of, 310
— statesmanship, 28
British-American League, 111
Brown, George, 95, 114, 118, 123, 124, 135, 136
Bruce, C. L. Cumming, 41, 79, 129
— — Elgin's letters to, 85, 91, 101, 107, 110, 114, 130, 132, 134, 220
Bruce, Frederick, 78, 245, 246, 253, 264, 273, 275
Bulwer, Sir Henry, 158, 161, 165
— — letter to Elgin, 161

Burke, Edmund, on E.I. Company, 21

Canada, 25–7, 78–191. (*See* also under ELGIN)
— fisheries, 158, 168, 169, 171, 172, 174, 186
— growing wealth and expansion of, 152
— political parties in, 92
— problems of, 83
— races and religions of, 80
Canning, Earl, 34, 207, 209, 210, 276, 278, 285, 290, 291, 294, 298, 299, 310
Canton, 197, 201, 208, 215–8, 236
Chamberlain, Sir Neville, 284, 308
China, Missions to, 194, 245
— joint expedition (with France) to, 253–5
— situation in, 194–206, 245–55
— treaty ports in, 197
— Treaty of Tientsin with, 227
China Correspondence, I, 194 *n*, 203, 204
  II, 206, 207, 211, 213, 223, 237, 241, 242
  III, 253, 258, 260, 261, 269

313

INDEX

314

INDEX

Elgin—*In Canada :*

Canadian problems in 1847, 80
political events, 92
political groups, 92–7
harnessed up with divided ministry, 97
on tour in western province, 98
first venture in genuine self-government, 99
conciliation, 101
Rebellion Losses Bill, 108
Montreal insults, 109
working for the future, 111
beginning to reap fruits of statesmanship, 112
creation of new moderate party, 115
railways, 117, 133, 148
Church and State in Canada, 122–7
Clergy Reserves Bill passed, 143
works for government by moderates, 132
visit to Boston, U.S.A., 151
advocates reciprocity treaty with U.S.A., 155
long negotiations, 162
visits Washington, 176
signs Reciprocity Treaty, 176
programme of reforms completed, 188
travels in Canada, 190

China and Japan :

arrives at Hong Kong, 208, 211
demands reforms and compensation, 216
sets up *de facto* government in Canton, 217

Elgin—*China and Japan :*

move to North China, 213
fall of Taku forts, 221
advance to Tientsin, 222
Treaty of Tientsin signed, 225
visits Japan and signs treaty, 232
returns to Shanghai, 236
more trouble with Chinese, 236
goes up Yangtze river, 240
leaves for England, 241

Second Mission to China:

arrives at Hong Kong, 257
at Tientsin, 262
capture of Peking, 263
burning of summer palace, 270
treaty and convention ratified, 273
sails for England, 275

In India :

earlier visit to Calcutta, 207
perception of Indian problems, 277
arrives in India, 277
machinery of government, 279
finance, 281, 299
eternal problem of N.W. frontier, 283, 303–7
attitude to Indians, 284
friction in government, 289
position of Viceroy, 290
a " little war," 307
death of Elgin, 308
work done in India, 309
place in British Imperial history, 7, 310

315

INDEX

For Lord Elgin's letters to C. L. Cumming Bruce and Lady Elgin *see* under those names

For letters and reports of Lord Elgin *see* under Clarendon, Earl of; Derby, Earl of; Gladstone, W. E.; Grey, Earl; Grey, Sir George; Malmesbury, Earl of; Newcastle, Duke of; Russell, Earl; Wood, Sir Charles

Elgin, Lady, Letters to, 23, 41, 89, 136, 137, 190, 191, 207, 208, 212, 217, 219, 220, 221, 223, 225, 233, 236, 241, 249, 256, 259, 260, 264, 275, 277

Emigration from U.K., 14–16

Europe in 1848, 101

Europeans in China, 212

— in India, 277

Foreign Office instructions to Elgin, 173

Free Trade in U.K., 153

French Canadians, 40, 81, 88, 92, 93, 107, 109, 115, 124, 135, 139

Frere, Sir Bartle, 280, 281, 289, 291, 293, 294, 298–9, 305

Galt, Sir A. T., 149

Gladstone, W. E., 36, 77, 119, 131, 145, 243, 244

— — letters of Elgin to (quoted), 46, 75, 77

Grant, Sir Hope, 253, 255, 260, 274

Granville, Earl, 194, 244, 276

Grey, Earl, 29, 77, 87, 99, 118, 120, 126, 149, 193

— — letters to Elgin (quoted), 100, 120, 126, 149

— — letters and reports of Elgin to, 78, 98, 102, 105, 114, 115, 116, 117, 120, 125, 126, 151, 154, 155, 159, 166

Grey, Sir George (of Fallodon), 136, 285

Grey, Sir George (Governor), 8, 31

— — letters of Elgin to, 136, 138, 140

Growth of population and trade in Britain after 1815, 13

Harvey, Sir John, 87

Hayti, 63

Head, Sir E., letter to (quoted), 143

Herbert, Sidney, 34, 253, 276

Hincks, Francis, 92, 94, 104, 116, 117, 118, 127, 129, 132, 133, 134, 138, 140, 150, 169, 173, 181

Hope, Admiral, 245–6

India, 25, 276–308. (*See* also under ELGIN)

— a land of problems, 278

— machinery of government of, 279–81, 289

— " troubled peace " after the Mutiny, 278

Irish immigrants in Canada, 81, 85, 98, 100

Jamaica, 43–77. (*See* also under ELGIN.)

— negroes of, 45–50, 68, 69, 70

Japan, 194, 226; visit of Elgin to, 231–6

316

INDEX